Marie

COUSINS

Family portrait

COUSINS

A MEMOIR

ATHOL FUGARD

WUP WITWATERSRAND UNIVERSITY PRESS

Witwatersrand University Press
1 Jan Smuts Avenue
Johannesburg
2001 South Africa

First published 1994

ISBN 1 86814 278 7

Typeset by The Penrose Press, Johannesburg
Printed by Clyson Printers (Pty) Ltd, Maitland

ACKNOWLEDGEMENTS

The author wishes to thank Pat Tucker, my editor at Witwatersrand University Press, who is responsible for the fiction that I know how to write prose.

Witwatersrand University Press acknowledges with thanks the contribution of Glenda Swart in collecting the photographs used in this book.

The Children of Sánchez by Oscar Lewis is published by Secker & Warburg (1961). The translation of Cavafy's 'The City' comes from *The Penguin Book of Greek Verse,* edited and translated by Constantine A Trypanis (Penguin Books, 1971). © Constantine A Trypanis, 1971, reproduced by permission of Penguin Books Ltd. The Netsilik Eskimo is quoted in the preface to *Eskimo Poems from Canada and Greenland* translated by Tom Lowenstein (Allison and Busby, 1973). *Light On The Ancient Worlds* by Frithjof Schuon (translated by Lord Northbourne) is published by Perennial Books (1965).

FOREWORD

I remember my childhood as a time of secrets.

You always made the announcement that you had a secret in that taunting sing-song voice reserved for very special challenges in the school playground. 'I've got a secret! I've got a secret!' I can't remember any toy or plaything being as precious as that wonderfully mysterious 'something I know' which you only dared share with your very, very best friend, and even then only in whispers in a dark corner and after blood oaths of continued secrecy. The hushed reverence in which we wrapped and unwrapped our precious secrets revealed a recognition of their subtle power over our lives. Young as we are when we first start having them and locking them away inside ourselves, they are nevertheless a very serious business; they will exert a profound influence in determining the sort of man or woman we will grow up to be. I believe this to be particularly true of writers and their writing which is, after all, essentially a trade in secrets. It is certainly so in my case. In one way or another, and in a variety of disguises, everything I have written has been an attempt to share secrets with you, either as the reader you are at this moment or as a past member of an audience at one of my plays. This little memoir is yet another attempt at sharing, and the secret this time is possibly the best kept of all those I've ever had. I make that claim for it because if it hadn't been for a chance reunion in Cape Town with one of my cousins, whom I hadn't seen for forty years, I doubt whether even I would have known I had it.

I must be careful though not to raise false expectations in you. It was hidden away for so long not because it was the biggest and best, the most shocking of them all – it is in fact only average as secrets go – but simply in order to protect a very delicate dynamic in my writing from premature and crude examination, particularly my own. Secrets have an ambiguous nature, however, and as important as it is to lock them away safely, so also is the compulsion to share them. A very necessary skill for a writer is the ability to judge when that moment has come. I know it is time now to share this one, which is the story of my relationship with two cousins – Johnnie and Garth – and the major role they played in my evolution as a writer. It is in any case not true that secrets are safe in the grave. Unlike our bones, they are not biodegradable. They can be dug up intact long after everything else has gone the way of dust unto dust. The vast unearthing of secrets by the scholarship of contemporary biography is ample proof of that.

One thing more. At any one moment in our lives we are all in the middle of a multiplicity of stories, all of them being spun out at the same time and woven together to form its fabric. *Cousins* is only one of the many threads that went in this fashion into the making of my childhood. Thus for example, in the years covered by this story of my two cousins, I was also living out the one of my relationship with Sam and Willie, which I tried to tell in fictional terms in *Master Harold ... and the Boys*. Those two beautiful men hardly figure, however, in the pages that follow. Similarly, there is only a hint of what are unquestionably the biggest and best of the stories of my childhood: those about my mother and my father. I am not yet up to telling them.

Sneeuberg Lodge
New Bethesda
November 1993

1

FAMILY PHOTO

This photograph has been hanging on walls in my life for all the time there is between me, as I sit writing these words at the age of sixty-one, and that little boy squatting on the bottom step on the extreme right. I think he is seven years old. Harold Athol Lanigan Fugard according to the birth certificate – but as far as the family was concerned, I was just plain 'Hally'. I changed all of that six or seven years later when I bullied, blackmailed, and bribed everyone into calling me Athol, a small but possibly significant act of rebellion. My dad's name was also Harold, and I wanted to be different. In the fifty years that this photo has been around I don't think I have given it so much as five minutes of my attention until now. I don't even know how it has managed to hang around for that long. By and large I've done a pretty good job of keeping my life uncluttered with relics and reminders of the past. It is something I do deliberately and very methodically. I spend very little of my life going back in time. Strolls down memory lane have absolutely no appeal for me, in fact, I avoid them as much as possible. In spite of this, there it was hanging patiently on a wall of the 'old house' in New Bethesda a few months ago, when my idea of writing a small memoir about my childhood crystallised and became a firm intention. It occurred to me that it could provide a perfect starting point for the memoir. I hurried around from the 'new house' to collect it, hurried back with it to my desk, propped it up and waited for it to write an opening paragraph.

It didn't. The harder I tried to get into it in the hope of finding a starting point for the story I wished to tell, the harder it became to connect myself in any way to that split second fifty and more years ago when the camera shutter clicked in front of 36 Clevedon Road, Port Elizabeth. It was very frustrating, particularly because I normally have a very easy and rich time with photographs. Like the great Chinese painter in the legend, I have no trouble in finding my way into them and disappearing. But that was not the case with this one. After a whole morning of trying, those sixteen faces were still staring, scowling and smiling back at me, and not letting me into any of their secrets. The reason for my difficulty was that my own intensely specific and intimate memory of those sixteen people – I can't place the dog – just didn't tally with the faces they had put on that day for the camera. I mean, that severe, square-jawed woman in the middle row, the one to the right of the gentle old lady … my mother? Good heavens no. The magnificent monument of a woman I remember was grey, a little stoop-shouldered toward the end, and very tired after a long and hard life, but in spite of all that she was still laughing at the follies and essential absurdity of existence, and raging against the injustices she saw around her in South Africa. You would have an easier time squeezing blood out of a stone than tickling a giggle out of the woman in the photo, which I could never resist doing to my mother right into my adulthood. But no, the voice of photographic reality insists: 'That *is* your mother, and next to her is your paternal grandmother, and on *her* right your Aunt Ann' … and so on and so on until finally '… and that is you there on the bottom step'.

But surely I can at least remember that occasion for which we had all obviously dressed up in our 'best'? My grandmother's birthday perhaps? A wedding anniversary? It was obviously a very auspicious family gathering, and there was no doubt a slap-up meal somewhere along the way, with my dad and my cousin Rhona, who had a wonderful singing voice and is standing demurely bonneted in the back row, providing the entertainment. Not a bit of it. I haven't been able to find a single personal memory to match it. In fact, that is really no surprise, of all my faculties, my memory is the most irrational. To this day I still find myself amazed at the seemingly irrelevant images it has jealously hoarded from the past, and the major front-page headline events it has chosen to forget completely.

The house in 'very respectable' Clevedon Road – 'comfortable and protected years'

But there is no arguing away the evidence of that photograph. We were all obviously there on the steps leading up to the front door. I can't even give it a rough date – and I must accept that the powerful, determined woman I have pointed out in the middle row, is indeed my mother. But if that stern young face doesn't tally with my memory of her, the strength of character it suggests certainly does. Looking at that photograph with the advantage of hindsight, it would seem from her determined, almost grim expression that she already sensed something of what the future had in store for her. There were hard years, and many of them, ahead. She was going to need all the resources of her strong Afrikaner stock to cope with her responsibilities as breadwinner of a family of three demanding children and an invalid husband. And am I reading more into it than is really there, or can one also see a hint of her powerful ambition? The Potgieters of Knoffelsfontein in the Middelburg, Cape district were simple, down to earth folk. My mother told me many times that although her education had only taken her as far as Standard Seven, she had been determined to 'better herself', as she put it. Falling in love with and then marrying a Fugard, a well-known and respected Port Elizabeth name, fitted perfectly into that agenda.

5

The author with Aunt Ann and his mother, sisters with 'a glorious capacity for laughter'

I can see that ambition in her face because I know it so well and owe it so much. Frustrated eventually, by the circumstances of her marriage, in achieving for herself all that she had hoped for, she transferred it and it became the driving force in mine. It never let me down. From my earliest childhood it was there as a support system for all the precocious and strange impulses of my life. Ten years old, and I wanted a 'double adult' subscription for the Port Elizabeth Public Library so that I could get at *all* the sections and not just the juvenile, and take out *twice* as many books …?? No problem. The money was forthcoming. Regardless of what the state of the family finances were, and they were very desperate on many occasions, my mother always found the fifteen shillings needed for the renewal. A few years later when I told her I wanted to go to university – the only Fugard to have done so – in like fashion no questions were asked. She simply set about begging, borrowing and adding a penny to the price of the doughnuts in the St George's Park Café so that when the time came she could get me on to the campus of the University of Cape Town.

6

And then at university ... two months before my final exams for a BA Degree which I believe I would have passed brilliantly having collected class medals for my subjects in the previous years – I wrote her a letter announcing my intention of throwing up my studies and hitch-hiking through Africa and around the world '... because that is what writers should do'. Back came her letter with its unwavering, and again unquestioning, support of my decision. It was an act of faith in my life that still takes my breath away. Ten years later, when I was married, with a child, and jobless, it was still there feeding me and my family – plates of food in a basket from the St George's Park Café – while I wrote an impossible play called *The Bloodknot*. And so on and on and on ... until the day she died.

On the other side of my grandmother is my Aunt Ann – Anna Potgieter, my cousin Johnnie's mother – another strong presence in my story. She was cast in the same mould as my mother, a strong-willed, independent spirit, and also very ambitious for her children. I suppose what I miss most in this photograph is even a small hint of their glorious capacity for laughter. The Afrikaner has a unique brand of dry, down-to-earth humour, and those two Potgieter sisters had more than their fair share of it. I have a stack of wonderful memories of their 'skinner en lag' sessions.

As far as my grandmother is concerned, I have only got one clear memory, and a hazy recollection. The memory is of standing next to her in the garden when she bent down to pull out a weed and farted ... virtually in my face. There was no apology, no comment. I interpreted it to be a particularly severe form of rebuke and because I had done nothing to deserve it, I burst into tears and ran into the house and hid away for the rest of the day. The hazy recollection is of my sister and myself skulking outside her locked bedroom door while inside she fed sweets to my brother Royal, her favourite. My mother told me once that if my grandmother had had her way my sister and I would never have seen the light of day. Because of my dad's infirmity, she felt that my mother should have limited the family to only one child.

And there he is behind her, one of his crutches just visible. There were three sons, and my father – Harold David Lanigan Fugard – was

Grandmother Fugard (little trace here of the 'gentle, silver-haired English presence') and Elizabeth Magdalena, Fugard's mother

the youngest. He was crippled in his childhood when he fell down a ship's gangway during a voyage between Southampton and Cape Town. His hip was badly damaged, and by the time the ship reached port, his left leg had been permanently impaired. Do I recognise him in this picture? Yes and no. The externals are easy enough: fine-featured and well-groomed, something of a lady's man in fact, meticulous about his clothes and personal habits – a quality I most certainly have not inherited. Mr Fugard was in every sense of the word, a gentleman. But what surprised me about the young man I look at, is his strength and vigour, the sense of a life that has not yet been sapped of its vital force by the habit of dependence on others. That was to be his story and it started with his anxious, over-protective mother. It is an interesting irony that our mothers played such opposite roles in our two lives. My debt to him is also enormous. I had a very special relationship with my father about which I will have more to say later.

For the purpose of this memoir I must focus finally on the children sitting on the bottom step. Cousin Johnnie is in the middle, my brother Royal on his right and myself on his left. Next to Royal is my sister Glenda and next to me my cousin Joy. The only person I don't recognise in that line-up is myself. I feel no connection whatsoever with that little boy scowling back at the camera. This doesn't really surprise me; even now there are days when I don't relate to, and in fact find myself very disturbed by the face staring back at me in the bathroom mirror. I have no hesitation at all with the Johnnie I see in the photograph. It is the Johnnie I knew, the Johnnie I remember with needle-sharp clarity, the Johnnie I will be writing about. Our relationship only really started about six years after this photograph was taken, but when it did, Johnnie breezed back into my life with the same easy-going and generous nature which the camera has so clearly captured.

The story of the photograph didn't end, though, with it being just a collection of vaguely remembered faces from my childhood. There was another surprise in store for me, and it came when I switched modes from subjective to objective, when, instead of trying to 'get into it', I stepped back and gave myself a perspective on all those faces. When I did that it suddenly became clear what I was looking at. The image it presents of the gentle, silver-haired English presences of my paternal grandmother and my father – the only two adult Fugards in it – swamped by the four Afrikaner Potgieter sisters, their husbands and children, is a perfect expression of my cultural reality. I am a mongrel son of white South Africa's two dominant cultures … Afrikaner and English-speaking. As if to make very sure that there would be no mistakes on this score, my grandmother is very firmly sandwiched between the most formidable of those Potgieter sisters – Elizabeth Magdalena on the one side and Anna Cornelia on the other.

I have often described myself as an Afrikaner writing in English, and the older I get the more that seems to be the truth, that my English tongue is speaking for an Afrikaner psyche. Somewhere or other somebody is on record as having said that my plays were translated into English before they were written in their original language. Could I have written them in the first instance in Afrikaans? No. My command of that language is, sadly, not good enough. But maybe that is just as well, because I have a deep and passionate love of English.

Our branch of the very large Potgieter tribe comes from the Middelburg district of the Karoo – I believe the farm's name was Knoffelsfontein – and I was born in Middelburg. The family moved to Port Elizabeth when I was still very young and it is there that I grew up and where I have spent most of my writing life. I have, however, now returned – emotionally and physically – to the Karoo. About twenty years ago a chance set of circumstances led me to discover the little village of New Bethesda in the heart of the Sneeuberg Mountains. As the crow flies it is about fifty miles from where I was born. I bought a house there and I now think of that world as home. My sense of belonging there, of 'belonging to' it, is of an order I have never experienced anywhere else in my life. The village is a little oasis, and the lives of the people that live there are characterised by a simple but profound piety. The Karoo itself is an austere world that withers human vanities and conceits. I have described it as the most spiritual of all the South African landscapes.

But coming back to the photograph, there is another felicitous touch to it; its strong matriarchal focus. Looking at it you are left in no doubt: the women are all-powerful. That was certainly the reality as far as our branch of the Fugards was concerned. As I remember it from the atmosphere in our Clevedon Road home, my grandmother was the head of the family. All decisions, all control of family economics were hers, and after her death my mother took over and her word became law. I believe the same was true of my Aunt Ann and her family. These two Potgieter sisters were both very powerful women, and I think this provoked something of a rivalry between them just as much as, at another level, it bonded them.

This dominance of the women in my early family life set a pattern for the rest of it. My relationships with women have always been the decisive

Cousin Garth, a schoolboy in Rhodesia
– 'a lonely and confused childhood'

and sustaining ones. I don't mean to diminish or sound careless of the important and loving relationship I had with my father, and the many male friendships I have had over the years, and continue to enjoy. It is just that there has always been an added dimension when it came to the women, which ended up making them my great companions and lovers, teachers and inspirers. I believe my writing reflects this. Whenever there is a woman present – a Lena, a Milly, a Hester, a Miss Helen, a Gladys Bezuidenhout – hers is always the dominant and affirmative voice.

I've tried, but without any success, to find an equivalent photograph of the Fugard family. Somewhere along the line there must surely have been a snapshot or a studio setup of my grandmother with her three sons. It would have been nice to balance the image of my cousin Johnnie, sitting at the base of that pyramid of Potgieters, with something similar for my Cousin Garth. They are the two heroes of my story. The best I can come up with is a snapshot of Garth in Rhodesia when he was a young man. This absence of an equivalent photo of the Fugards is very revealing of the difference between the two families; on the one hand the powerful tribal coherence of the Afrikaner, and on the other, the rugged individualism of the English.

Although I have no memories of the day on which the Family Photo was taken, I have plenty of other memories of gatherings of the Potgieter clan … anniversaries, weddings and funerals, with members sometimes travelling hundreds of miles to be present. By contrast, even during the years when the three Fugard sons were alive and living in the Eastern Cape, I don't remember a single family get-together. They were a family of individualists and they maintained very polite distances from each other.

In the course of a heated argument I had with my mother when I was about fifteen years old, with a stroke of literary precocity I categorised the three branches of the family as the snob Fugards – my Uncle Toop and his family; the wicked Fugards – my Uncle Garth and his family; and the frightened Fugards – my family. The argument between my mom and myself had been provoked by the prospect of another obligatory visit to the 'snob' Fugards in their posh seafront flat. My mother always insisted on dragging me along on these visits. I resented those Fugards keenly, not because of anything they had done to us but because visits always involved the sight of my mother kow-towing to our well-heeled relatives. Her fawning in the presence of the high and mighty was the one aspect of my mother's nature that angered me. I was jealous of her dignity and hated anything that compromised it. I don't doubt that I am being grossly unfair to that branch of the family, but the prejudice remains. To this day I still bridle at any suggestion of class distinction and privilege. And then the wicked Fugards – My Uncle Garth, his wife Dulcie, and my cousin Garth … interesting that he also started out with the burden of his father's name. The 'wickedness' belonged to the two men – my Aunt Dulcie was an angel – and what that 'wickedness' was all about is half of the story I am going to tell. And the 'frightened' Fugards? Yes, we were that. Always a little desperate economically, and struggling to make ends meet. Always at least a little frightened of wicked relatives, creditors and their ruthless demands, and ultimatums that had my mother scrambling around to find money to pay rent, and the bills that were always mounting up. I've inherited her capacity for pointless and excessive anxiety and worry. It has wasted a lot of my life's energy.

❏   ❏   ❏

Did Johnnie and Garth ever meet? I suppose it is possible, though I have no memory of ever seeing the two of them together. In any case if there was ever an encounter it had no consequences in my life. They had nothing in common and lived in completely separate worlds. But in an imaginative sense there was of course a meeting between those two worlds and their cultures, Afrikaner and English, in me. As I have already said, that is my reality and at one level, that is also what this story is all about.

I am going to deal with the two worlds separately because that is the way I experienced them and even though my earliest memories of Garth precede those of Johnnie, I am going to write about Johnnie first. It 'feels' right that way and 'feeling right' is one of the basic instincts that I follow as a writer.

2

JOHNNIE

My relationship with Johnnie is a story about two pianos and the journey I made between them, and how when the first one fell silent it was my profound good fortune to find the other. It was a journey of the imagination, and as such, the most important one I've ever made. In a sense it has never really ended. Everything I have written, all the plays that lie behind me, are at one level the milestones of the personal odyssey that started with those two pianos.

The first one was a splendid old Fritz Kuhla upright. You discovered the name, in gold-lettered Gothic script when you lifted up the keyboard cover and removed the length of green felt that protected the keys. This splendid old instrument was the glowing rosewood centrepiece of the lounge of the Jubilee Residential Hotel, and the man who played it was Harold David Lanigan Fugard, my father. The lounge itself was that only in name; there was nothing about the dark, gloomy room I remember that invited anything but the briefest stay in one of the sagging sofas or straight-backed chairs that stood around the walls. A notice above the archway leading into it announced that it was 'For The Use of Residents', but, apart from my dad's piano playing, the only other moment of life I remember in it was when my sister and I – ten and eight years old respectively – managed to coax a few reluctant boarders into the uncomfortable chairs for our performance of *Snow White and the Seven Dwarfs*. My sister was Snow White – I was everything else. For the rest the lounge was out of bounds to us children unless my dad was at the piano.

But getting him to it wasn't by any means an easy exercise. By the time we took over the Jubilee he had become increasingly reluctant to sit down at it and play, and when he did you could almost feel the inertia he had to overcome before lifting his hands to the keyboard. It was as if forty years of holding on to his crutches had blunted and coarsened them, drained them of their music-making magic. So the timing of a request was very important. I eventually realised that the best moment to try was when he came back from a session in one of the Main Street bars, and the deeper the session had been, the better my chances. When that was the case a hearty 'Come along chum, let's go tickle the ivories for a bit' usually did the trick. Even so there would always still be a mildly murmured protest that his playing days were over, but I knew that he could be bullied past that moment and into the lounge. Once at the piano, habit took over. I can still see his little manoeuvre as clearly as if it had happened yesterday: the way he would ease himself off his crutches, then steadying himself with one hand on the top of the piano, lean them against the wall, and on one leg swing himself down on to the piano stool. After a few 'warm-up' chords and a couple of runs up and down the keys he would settle down to 'tickling the ivories' for an hour or so, and Hally, standing on his left and turning the pages of the dog-eared old dance music albums for him, would be in heaven.

The names alone are still music in my ears: 'Ramona', 'Silver Threads Among the Gold', 'Bye-Bye Blackbird', 'Harbour Lights', 'When the Red Red Robin' ... and at least a score of others that I never tired of hearing even when his hands began to fumble the chords and strike wrong notes. I knew the words of all the songs by heart and used to sing along while he played. My all-time-never-to-be-forgotten favourite was 'Mona', a ballad about a cowboy who had to shoot his horse:

> 'I've only got five bullets in my old six-shooter
> 'cause I had to say goodbye to Mona ...'

... words I could never sing without a lump in my throat and tears in my eyes. I still remember the melody.

Thinking back on it now I realise that it was during those golden hours in that dark room that I first savoured what were to become the two great addictions of my life – words and music. And it was probably there also that my dad and I forged the special bond between us that kept us 'chums' up to the day he died. For both of us those sessions at the piano were interludes of soul-comfort in the generally troubled, anxious and noisy life of our years in the Jubilee. I also have a few cherished memories of other but very different 'golden hours' with my father. They too are in the Jubilee, but this time late at night. My father is in bed and I am sitting in a chair at his bedside. The cramps in the stump of his gammy leg – which had him whimpering all through his life – are particularly bad, and I am massaging it with Oil of Wintergreen and Embrocation. His groans have woken me up and I have got out of bed to help. We have lit a candle so as not to disturb the others – the boarding house must have been full because the five of us were all bedded down in the one room. Then when the pain has subsided and I am just sitting there, staring into the golden cobwebs which drowsy eyes spin around candle-flames, he on his side rewards me by 'spinning out a yarn'. It is not an original. What I listen to enthralled is a potted version of one of the great stories of his youth – Sherlock Holmes, *Call of the Wild, Frankenstein, Dracula, The Hound of the Baskervilles.*

And then yet another image of the two of us together. This time we are strolling along Chapel Street to or from the Opera House Cinema where one shilling and threepence had bought us a ticket for the latest offering from Hollywood. We both loved the monster movies – *Frankenstein, Dracula, The Mummy, The Wolfman* – though I always closed my eyes at the really scary parts. Walking home slowly afterwards along the quiet street, we would discuss and cast a critical eye on what we had just seen. The key phrases were: 'I didn't believe that part where he …' and 'what they should have done was …' and we would then dismantle the story, examine its bits and pieces, and reassemble them to our liking. It was all about stories, you see, and telling them, and those sessions with my dad were probably my first lessons in the craft.

My dad was being honest, though, when he said he had passed his prime as a pianist. That had been before I was born, when his dance band 'The Orchestral Jazzonians' was the most sought after in the Eastern Cape for wedding receptions, dances and parties. In my

The Orchestral Jazzonians with Harold Fugard poised to 'tickle the ivories'

scratching around for information for this memoir, I came across a photograph of the Jazzonians from that period of glory in his early manhood. My mother never tired of telling me the story of how, when she first came to Port Elizabeth from Middelburg, she fell in love with a handsome young man who played the piano in the Palmerston Hotel Lounge, and ended up marrying him. The room in which she was living at the time was above the old Rand Café in Jetty Street and from her window she could see him at the piano in the hotel lounge. At night she used to put off the light in her room, open the window and lie in the dark listening to his music. Looking at the photograph one can't but agree with her: he certainly was a handsome young man, and in spite of all that was to happen to him, there was never any coarsening of those fine features. The same could be said for his manner. He remained a perfect gentleman until the day he died.

Sadly, those golden moments at the piano were not fated to last. As my dad's musicianship continued its decline, my own appetite for music grew. Standing there next to him in the lounge, turning the pages and singing, I began to get impatient, and not just with his fumbled playing. Much as I loved the old favourites I wanted to hear some new ones. But whenever a likely looking title came up as we paged our way through the albums he would shake his head and make me page on. If I insisted – 'Come on chum, give it a go!' – he would sigh, squint at the music for a second or two, try a few chords or a whisp of melody, then shake his head and murmur something about it being too much for him now. Those sessions in the Jubilee lounge were his swan-song. During his last years there was in fact no longer a piano in his life. On my side the frustration was acute and would eventually lead to piano lessons and an attempt to master the instrument for myself. But that was still some time away. Fortunately for me, in terms of my immediate needs, my Uncle Lou and Aunt Ann decided to sell their small dairy business in Pretoria and move down to Port Elizabeth, and with them came my cousin Johnnie who was by then a qualified fitter and turner.

My memory of Johnnie starts with a head of rich, wavy jet-black hair that I can't ever remember seeing untidy. It was responsible for the exciting perfumed aura that always surrounded him, especially on Saturday nights when a generous dollop of Brylcream, Bay Rum or Vitalis provided the finishing touch to his toilet. Johnnie was inoffensively vain, always well-groomed and with an engaging sense of himself as 'the charmer'. He was quite simply everything I wanted to be when I grew up and I hero-worshipped him, my adoration being expressed by that highest of all forms of flattery, imitation. I imitated his laugh – a deep throated chortle that bubbled out whenever he teased somebody – my mother being one of his favourite targets; I imitated the way he spoke and his speech mannerisms; I imitated the way he walked … and I followed him everywhere. When I think back on it now I am amazed that I can't remember a single harsh word from him, because heaven knows, a doting, clinging little slave the likes of myself would certainly have got on my nerves. But there it is: this darkly handsome twenty-one-year-old young man quite happily let his short-trousered, freckle-faced little cousin tag along on all his adventures.

But apart from his good looks and his gentle, fun-loving soul that was ever obliging of the many favours my mother asked of him, there was something else about Johnnie that would have drawn me to him even if he had in fact been as objectionable as he was likeable. Johnnie was music. It was his passion as much as mine, and he made it on both the piano and the violin. My Aunt Ann had looked after his musical talents – and they were considerable – in the same way that my mother would eventually nurse my literary aspirations. But the full significance of all that was to come later. Our relationship started off being one of fun and games and the youthful quest for adventure and romance in the milkbars of Main Street and the beach front promenade of Humewood.

❏ ❏ ❏

The first setting for our relationship was the world of smallholdings and scabby little farms along what is now the 'old' Cape Road. My Aunt Ann and Uncle Lou had put their savings into one of them – a fifty morgen parcel of land on which they planned to grow flowers and vegetables for the market. A year or so later we followed them, selling the Jubilee and moving out onto Devon, a twenty morgen plot a mile or so further out along the Cape Road. Thinking about it now there really was no sense at all in that move. Apart from one or two juvenile efforts on my side, no serious attempt was ever made to work our land and live off it the way my uncle and aunt were doing. All of my mom's energies, and she was the family generator, were going into the recently acquired St George's Park Tea Room. It had replaced the Jubilee as our source of income and was to remain that, and my mom's pride and joy, for the next thirty years.

Being that far out of town made life very complicated for all of us. The only public transport was a very basic bus service run by a local Chinese shop owner. This consisted of an old rattletrap with wooden bench-style seating which clattered into town in the early morning and back in the early evening. For the rest we were dependent on the family Ford V8 which was getting on in years and breaking down quite often. My brother and I also had the option of bicycles, and we were forced to use them quite often. The only reason I can think of now for moving those sixteen miles out of town into a cold and comfortless little house was my mother's Afrikaner instinct to be on the land, reinforced by the bond of love and rivalry between the two sisters. If Anna could sit on her stoep and smile at her fifty morgen, so also could Elizabeth Magdalena.

Athol and Glenda, father and the Ford V8 'which was getting on in years and breaking down quite often'

As it turned out neither sister did much sitting on the stoep or smiling. They were desperate times. For both families that 'return to the land' turned out to be a big mistake. After only two years of it on Devon, we moved back into the city and we were followed a year or so later by my aunt, uncle and Johnnie.

But brief as that time might have been, it has left me with images of a little world that was as unique and rich in detail as anything else I have experienced in my life. In 1946 sixteen miles along the Cape Road meant you had left the bright lights of civilisation very far behind. There was no telephone or electricity on Devon, and for water we were dependent on rainwater tanks. The very basic lifestyle created by these

The younger Fugard siblings with mother and the family car

conditions – woodburning stove in the kitchen and candles in the bedrooms – was typical of all the smallholdings along the Cape Road. It was a very humble world. The simple houses – most of them made of corrugated iron – were occupied by working-class Afrikaner families. I got to know those people well from those early morning bus rides into town. By the time we reached the Hunter's Retreat Hotel – the half-way mark – the bus had a full load of sleepy-eyed men and women of all ages, clutching thermos flasks and lunch tins and fogging up the bus windows with their breath and cigarette smoke. They were headed for the railways, the post office and the factories of Port Elizabeth – GM, Ford and Firestone, among others – which provided them with their livelihood. What I realise now of course is that in studying my fellow passengers with furtive fascination I was feeling my way for the first time into that very specific world of the alienated working-class Afrikaner. It is one that has always fascinated me, and my play *Hello and Goodbye* is my personal celebration of it. I had Johnnies and Hesters sitting all around on those bone-crunching, gear-grinding early morning rides into town.

My exploration of the world around Devon was a huge adventure and every bit as exciting as my conquest of Main Street had been during our years in the Jubilee. To start with it was, and in every possible way, completely different. Instead of back streets and shop windows I was now exploring groves of bluegum and Port Jackson willow where it was still possible to surprise the occasional duiker. Out in the fynbos veld an afternoon ramble usually included at least one good 'skrik' when a flock of guinea fowl or francolin rose raucously from underfoot. It was here that I discovered that there was more to birds – eventually to become a life-long hobby – than feral pigeons shitting on Queen Victoria's statue. Cape Road itself was then still the main road link to the Western Cape, but apart from its tarmac surface it had little in common with the Main Street I had come to know so well. Instead of dodging motor cars, trams and buses, or weaving my way like a little minnow through the currents of Saturday shoppers, I was walking or cycling leisurely next to the donkey carts and ox wagons loaded with firewood that were making their way back slowly to the city's locations. The loss of my weekly bioscope treat had been compensated for by the stick fights of the Xhosa kwadins (uncircumcised youths) on the St Albans corner on Sunday afternoons. These mock fights, as regular as any matinée showing, looked real enough to me. To my huge admiration, and that of the young Xhosa boys, my brother Royal eventually took part, which made watching them every bit as exciting as a good thriller or western. I can still hear clearly the sound of one of those sticks landing on flesh in a well-aimed and well-timed blow. Royal got his fair share of them, and he took them without flinching.

Back at home the adult conversations on which I eavesdropped also underwent a radical change. Instead of it being all boarding house talk about residents' complaints and servant troubles, now when the two sisters got together for 'koffie and skinner' it was to talk about seeds and seasons and good kraal manure, with the two of them trying their best to recall what their father had done to get the marvellous vegetables they remembered coming out of his garden in Middelburg. I listened with fascination to the names of flowers I hadn't heard of before … lupin and delphinium, phlox and stocks, gladioli and dahlias. Johnnie's discovery of the box of seeds in *Hello and Goodbye*, and his delight as he reads out the names, is a celebration of those fragrant hours when my mother and my Aunt Ann gave me my first lessons in loving the earth.

I find it so easy to understand the attempt those two Potgieter sisters made to return to the land after their urban adventures. That deep instinct in the Afrikaner to root himself in a piece of land that is his own and which can feed him and his family is a powerful element in my own psychology – more so, the older I get. The fruit trees and vegetable akkers of Sneeuberg Lodge, my home in the Little Karoo hamlet of New Bethesda, the windmill at the bottom of the garden, with its steady supply of life-sustaining water, are what now make New Bethesda 'home' in my life. The bag of walnuts I harvest every year from the old walnut tree next to the windmill means more to me than any theatre award I've received.

I remember particularly two incidents on Devon that have had resonances all through my life and which capture something of the folly of our brief sojourn 'on the land'. Ignorant as I was about everything connected with the earth and husbanding it, my little Afrikaner soul smelt the potential of those fallow acres behind the house. I knew they could be made to produce – after all my Aunt Anna and Uncle Lou weren't doing so badly down the road – and I set about trying to make that happen. I had overheard Aunt Ann use the magic word 'strawberries' and my youthful imagination went to work, conjuring up visions of bushel loads of ripe, red berries. My mother, whose hugely impressionable nature I had inherited, was easily seduced by my vision, and so in due course a couple of hundred strawberry seedlings arrived in the boot of the old Ford. The early spring day I had chosen for the planting turned out to be a bad one – bitterly cold winds and lashing rain – but with a youthful display of the obstinacy that has been responsible for so much misery in my life, I refused to change my plans. The bad weather also meant that there were no other volunteers, so I had to do it alone. I ended up spending the day alternately in short stretches on my haunches out in the land planting the seedlings in mud, and long stretches thawing out in front of the wood stove in the kitchen which I kept well stoked all day long. When the last one was in, I stood up in the muddied and completely sodden old overcoat I was wearing, and looked back over my handiwork. The rows of young strawberry seedlings stretched away in the still pelting rain as crooked as a dog's hind leg. I'd never watched any actual planting before and the idea of pegging out your line with a length of twine just hadn't occurred to me.

Straight lines have been a problem all my life. About ten years after the strawberry episode I found myself in the South Pacific. I was working my way around the world as a deck hand on an old tramp steamer. One day when we were steaming between Fiji and the Gilbert Islands, the first mate invited me to have a go at the wheel. After forty-five minutes of my trying to keep a steady course on the compass in front of me, he tapped me on the shoulder and took me out onto the bridge. Wordlessly he pointed to the stern. The frothy, churned-up wake of the ship stretching away over a very blue Pacific was every bit as crooked as that line of strawberry seedlings. I eventually got the knack of it however and in fact took the tub – the SS Graigaur (Welsh for rock of gold) – through the Panama Canal.

But back on Devon ... absolutely nothing came of those strawberry seedlings and my day in the rain and mud. However, not all my attempts at gardening were unsuccessful. I tried my hand at flowers as well, and it is in this area that I chalked up a few impressive successes: a bank of tall gladioli that were actually splendid enough to sell in the tearoom, and on the side of the house one summer a bed of zinnias that even my Aunt Ann, who never handed out praise lightly, conceded were special. I cherish a memory of my dad standing on his crutches in early morning sunlight, admiring them in all their glory. It is an appropriately gentle image.

My dad was also a spectator in the second of the two incidents I mentioned. I can't remember how it happened, but the two of us were alone in the house for the day, moping around and looking for something to do. It must have been particularly irksome for him to be marooned sixteen miles away from his Main Street haunts. He was an out-and-out townsman and had no sense of the land or anything connected with it.

Devon fronted directly onto the Cape Road and along the boundary fence was a line of bluegum trees, the only trees on the property.

Heaven alone knows where the idea came from, but there I was suddenly, standing in front of my dad with a large wood axe. 'Chum, I'm going to chop down those trees.' And that is what I proceeded to do, with my dad standing on the stoep and giving me moral support and a round of applause every time I shouted 'Timber!' when one of the trees came crashing down. I think there were about eight of them. Giving myself a generous, self-satisfied rest and a chat with my dad on the stoep in between each one, I got through the whole day in this fashion. I was very proud of myself for having enough savvy to assault them in such a way that they fell inside the property and not across the fence and the road. I eagerly awaited my mom's return home at the end of the day so that I could also revel in her approval of my handiwork. When it came, her reaction of horror and the deepest distress took me completely by surprise. Standing at the garage and looking in the direction of the fallen trees, I could see she was on the point of tears. A scorching flush of anger, disappointment and shame that I can still feel, passed over me. 'I didn't know you loved them!' I blurted out, and then burst into tears. In that one instant she had made me realise just how terrible a thing I had done. It was a lesson that I have never forgotten and it has invested trees with a quality that has made them very real 'presences' all through my life.

I have never been more conscious of this than here in New Bethesda where I am working on this memoir. It is winter up here now and my days usually end with a muffled-up late night walk through the village. Lights are usually out and everyone is asleep at that hour. But not the trees, the magnificent pines and cypresses, poplars and bluegums, acacias and wild pear that line the dusty roads of the village. The sense of them alive and awake, their huge black presences magnified still further by the night, is quite awesome. I have come to know and respect them individually as much I do the people of the valley. They offer a very real companionship in that late, frost-sharp hour.

The bonding that started between Johnnie and myself at that time is neatly captured in a snapshot by that now extinct species, the candid

Hally and Johnnie – the bond captured in a snapshot by
a street photographer

street photographer. In the years that I am writing about we had a
couple of them in Port Elizabeth, and they plied their trade in Main
Street and the Humewood Beachfront promenade. Their technique was
the very essence of simplicity: stationed to one side of the pavement,
camera at the ready, they would spy out a likely approaching subject, and
then when you were in range and hopefully with a smile on your face,
the shutter would click and you would be handed a card as you strode
on past and which you presented when you collected your photograph a
few days later. My guess is that the one of Johnnie and myself was taken
on a Saturday morning. It's got that sort of purposeful energy about it.
Saturday morning, when the pavements were crowded with shoppers and

27

black hawkers, newspaper sellers and Bible thumping evangelists, was the high point in Main Street's weekly cycle. The photograph, which I used for the poster of the London production of *Master Harold ... and the Boys*, at the National Theatre, says a lot about the two of us and our relationship. Johnnie, studying a piece of paper in his hand, is his usual relaxed and good looking self, his shock of wavy black hair seen to its full advantage. The fact that his shirt collar is lifted out and folded back over the collar of his sports coat suggests a warm summer's day. Striding next to him is his doting little slave, an awkward and freckle-faced young Hally. Matters aren't helped by his ill-fitting clothes – a jacket and trousers that are already a size too small, and the khaki shirt with its crumpled collar. He is saying something to his cousin and his emotional dependence on the older man can be seen quite clearly in the body language of that moment, though I think it does also suggest an eager and willing disposition.

But what I find most telling about the photograph is the way in which it has captured, or at least hints at, the essential innocence of our relationship. During those Devon years there was no music in it, that was to come later with the move back into town. The first bond between us was quite simply the harmless mischief and good natured high jinks we schemed up in an attempt to give our rather ordinary lives the tingle of a little bit of excitement. Whether it was bareback donkey races out in the veld or trying to frighten the locals with ghostly, sheeted apparitions late at night, Johnnie's fertile imagination was never at a loss when it came to finding something new for us to try out. The most 'tingling' of all his ideas came one Guy Fawkes when a packet of ominous-looking 'Thunder Bangs' from the Chinese mainland inspired that imagination to new and very daring heights. They were ugly squat brown-paper fire-crackers that in my feverish imagination looked like miniature sticks of the real dynamite that was being thrown around in the adventure movies of those days. 'Time bombs' was the exciting phrase on Johnnie's lips, and the final product from his adept hands – three of them taped together and joined to a homemade fuse that was long enough for a getaway after lighting up.

Our first target was the Rand Café in Jetty Street. We sauntered in casually one evening, chose a corner table and ordered milkshakes. While sipping these we debated for the last time whether to proceed with the plan or not. I was scared stiff and all for calling it off. But not Johnnie. He had invested too much in the design of those bombs. So, with a lot of suppressed and very nervous giggling, we decided to go ahead. I was seated in such a way that I could watch the few other customers and the proprietor behind the counter while Johnnie, ostensibly bending down to pick up a spoon he had knocked off the table, placed the bomb. A few more swallows of milkshake to steady our nerves, and Johnnie lit the cigarette that was going to light the fuse. I waited for a moment when nobody was paying us any attention, and then gave Johnnie the agreed signal which, if I remember correctly, was to scratch my ear. We got up, and with our hearts in our mouths sauntered casually up to the counter, paid our bill and then ambled just as casually out into the night where we scuttled off to the getaway car – Johnnie's near vintage little red Austin. We had no sooner got in when the bomb went off. It was a very impressive bang and caused great consternation in the café, the agitated proprietor dashing out on to the pavement as we drove away.

Our second exploit was just as successful. This time we targeted the beach front promenade, the bomb being placed behind a rubbish bin near an ice cream kiosk. Watching from the other side of the road we saw a short queue of customers scattering in all directions when it went off. But in spite of the adrenalin charge we got from these two escapades, we also had serious misgivings. We knew we were playing with fire in more senses than one, and that something could quite easily go wrong. To my huge relief, and I think Johnnie's as well, we decided that there wouldn't be a third. Recalling this particular escapade has left me with an uneasy feeling. I wish now we had never thought it up. Innocent as our intentions might have been I can't help finding in it a small hint of the real time bombs that were one day going to punctuate our history with such devastating and tragic results.

The two of us were very atypical young South Africans in our total lack of interest in the nation's unofficial religion – sport. None of the major denominations – rugby, cricket or soccer – ever claimed us as followers. When it came to the need for a bit of healthy weekend exercise, we chased girls instead of balls, though we turned out to be rank amateurs at this sport as well. In the course of the hundreds of hours that we put into it I can remember us only once being successful in persuading a pretty member of the opposite sex to join us for a ride in the little Austin … that being the huge inducement we always offered. But we certainly tried. Our favourite haunts were milkbars – particularly the Willowtree which had an irresistible parfait special called a Knickerbocker Glory, a veritable Everest of different coloured ice creams with glaciers of hot chocolate sauce – the beach front promenade and Happy Valley. During the Christmas season there was also Playland, the funfair which used to visit Port Elizabeth during the holidays. The two of us, eternal optimists to the end, would methodically make the rounds, trying to catch a pretty girl's eye. Or more accurately, Johnnie would. My role was to bolster up his courage, give him a push from behind as it were – 'Go on man, she's smiling at you'. I would then take my pleasure vicariously when he worked up enough courage to saunter nonchalantly in her direction and start the chatting and chaffing that constituted the essential opening gambit of this most ancient of all sports.

Was my relationship with my cousin and the world in which I was growing up genuinely as innocent as I like to remember it? Or has my memory been blurred by time and nostalgia? I don't think so. I do believe that just as I, in the Blakean sense, passed from my songs of innocence to those of experience, so too did my world. There is just no comparison between what young people have to contend with today and the realities of my youth. There surely can't be any denying that their world is infinitely more complicated and dangerous than the one I had to negotiate. One of the most inspiring experiences of my adult life has been the privilege of witnessing how young South Africans of all race groups have resisted the attempts of a powerful and evil system to indoctrinate them with racial prejudice. The traditional and then still unofficial apartheid of my youth did not in any way mount the same massive assault on the young soul as was later to be the case with the twisted genius of Verwoerd's philosophy. It is not just a blind act of faith that sustains my belief in the future of our country; I have this tangible evidence that the evils of the past are not DNA molecules in our gene structure from which there is no escape.

❏ ❏ ❏

It was inconvenience more than anything else that finally forced my mom to move the family back into town. Our new home was a substantial and, by comparison with Devon's primitive facilities, luxurious piece of suburbia on the corner of Hudson Street and Third Avenue in Newton Park. In the case of my Aunt Ann and Uncle Lou, their move back into town about a year later was not so simple. Their farming venture had turned out to be a failure and left them embittered. I have a vague recollection of my mom feeling guilty about all of this because she had been partly responsible for their decision to sell their flourishing dairy in Pretoria and move back to Port Elizabeth. Their next venture was a small general dealer store on the Buffelsfontein Road in the area known as Salisbury Park. Johnnie of course moved with them and it is here, in the gloomy lounge of the house attached to the shop, that our relationship moved into its last and richest phase.

❏ ❏ ❏

I write, read or even just think the names 'Buffelsfontein Road' or 'Salisbury Park' and I smell a heavy fragrance compounded of paraffin and chew-tobacco, ground coffee and blue soap, all stirred into the clammy sweetness from sacks of moist brown sugar; I close my eyes and I see again a dimly lit world of shadows and muted, deferential voices as soft as the moths fluttering around an old Coleman lamp that is hissing away on a wooden counter. My Aunt Ann and Uncle Lou are behind it serving, with bad grace, the trickle of customers that come in out of a black night – there is also no electricity out here. Old men, tired women, barefoot little children – coloured, African and an occasional white – all of them poor, and living in the simple little houses scattered around the shop, clutching sixpences and tickeys and pennies for candles or bread, or the small brown paper-wrapped portions – I remember the word 'kadoosie' – of tea or sugar. In all of this there was nothing unique to Salisbury Park; there were at least another dozen little worlds exactly like it scattered around the candle and lamplit periphery of Port Elizabeth. Their names litter my plays: Veeplaas, Kleinskool, Korsten, Missionvale, Fairview, Swartkops ... a litany of names that Lena would one day turn into a mantra as she searched for the meaning of her life. All my life, and I don't really know why, it has been those humble and desperate little worlds that have fired my imagination; I have studied them and tried to imagine my way into their secret life as eagerly and passionately as others do with the palaces and mansions of the mighty.

In his important and moving study of the Mexican poor, *The Children of Sánchez*, the American anthropologist Oscar Lewis defined what he called the culture of poverty:

> To those who think the poor have no culture, the concept of a culture of poverty may seem like a contradiction in terms. It would also seem like an attempt to give poverty a certain dignity and status. This is not my intention. In anthropological usage the term culture implies, essentially, a design for living which is passed down from generation to generation. In applying this concept of culture to the understanding of poverty, I want to draw attention to the fact that poverty in modern nations is not only a state of economic deprivation, of disorganization, or the absence of something. It is also something positive in the sense that it has a structure, a rationale and defence mechanisms without which the poor could hardly carry on. In short it is a way of life ...

His book helped me to recognise the emotional and psychological coherence of the lives in those humble little worlds that so fascinated me. From my point of view however there was something else about that 'culture of poverty' which he didn't deal with, and that is the way in which the very destitution of those lives can sometimes invest simple things and events, even simple gestures, with huge archetypal values and resonances. When Lena breaks and shares a piece of brown bread with Outa as they sit huddled together in the cold of the Swartkops mudflats, it is the profound simplicity of those elements that turn that moment into a mass, a bitter celebration of her life.

Salisbury Park was a flowering of all these values and they were hothoused for me in the dark, fragrant interior of that shop. I got to

The St George's Park Tea Room, 'a place where we all came together to tie and untie that rosary of knots that is every family's unique story'

know it well as a result of regular Sunday night visits, at least two years of them, by my mom and myself – I can't remember my father, brother or sister ever going along. We used to drive out there after closing up the tea room in St George's Park, usually around 6pm. Making sure that the car was parked outside the shop in such a way that my Uncle Lou could keep an eye on it – according to him there were a lot of 'skelms' out there in the dark – we would troop off, led by my Aunt Ann with a paraffin lamp, into the even gloomier house at the back. After the obligatory session of 'koffie and skinner' we would settle back to enjoy a session of piano playing from Johnnie. Uncle Lou seldom joined us. He stayed behind in the shop, serving customers and stirring up the large pot of tripe and lights he was cooking for his dogs. He had ended up deeply disillusioned by human nature and now preferred the company of animals.

The lounge in which we did our socialising was the usual heavy-handed South African attempt at respectability; a Chesterfield suite of elephantine proportions, one or two grim family portraits on the walls, and an ailing fern in a stand in a corner. We had an equally dead room in the Newton Park house. But like their predecessor in the Jubilee

Residential Hotel, both lounges were redeemed by the dark glowing presence of a piano. Johnnie never needed any coaxing to sit down at it; he loved his music – and applause – too much to be coy about it.

My relationship with Johnnie at the piano was very different from the physically intimate one I had had with my father. I never stood beside him, one arm over his shoulders, turning the pages and singing along the way I had done with my dad in the lounge of the Jubilee. At first I was just another passive member of his audience like my mother and my aunt, sunk back deep into one of those carnivorous club easies, while he played. But it didn't stay that way for long. His music was far too potent. It stirred up wonderfully turbulent feelings inside me and the impulse to do something with them, to release them in some way, became overpowering. A decisive factor in all this was Johnnie's repertoire as a pianist. It did not consist solely of popular music the way my father's had. As it happened he would eventually also end up as a very successful band leader in his own right, but at this early point in his musical career he was still exploring the world of music and he took me along with him on his voyages of discovery. The Chopin nocturnes and études, Debussy, Rachmaninoff, Brahms and Schubert, are just a few of the memorable landfalls we made together. And what amazing discoveries they were! They didn't only stir up my yeasty adolescence in the way my dad's sentimental ballads had done, they were like actual places, gardens of delight in which my imagination roamed freely. The wonderful event inside me, the emotional journey I found myself making as Johnnie's hands travelled up and down the keyboard demanded their own unique life. All I had then with which to respond is all I have ever had and out of which I have fashioned all of my responses to life ... words. This is how a Netsilik Eskimo man described the mysterious transformative impulse that turns thought and feeling into words:

'A person is moved like an ice-flow which drifts with the current. His thoughts are driven by a flowing force when he feels joy, when he feels fear, when he feels sorrow. Thoughts can surge in on him, causing him to gasp for breath, and making his heart beat faster. Something like a softening of the weather will keep him thawed. And then it will happen that we, who always think of ourselves as small, will feel even smaller.

And we will hesitate before using words. But it will happen that the words that we need will come of themselves. When the words that we need shoot up of themselves – we have a new song.'

In my case the result wasn't song, but story and it was in that little room on the Buffelsfontein Road that I made my first attempt at that most ancient of all the arts.

I wish I could remember the specific little accidents that led to Johnnie and me evolving the performance pieces that eventually became the main and public event of those Sunday evenings. I'm sure there would be a lesson there about the craft of story-telling. But all I can recall now is the final process. It went like this: I would sit back, listen to the music, and wait for the first image. It always came, and when it did I would turn it into words, and then develop and elaborate it, improvising as I went along with the music. I was in a sense translating the music into words – the music always leading. But it wasn't long before a major development took place that reversed this order of things. What we discovered was that once started, my stories were inclined to have a life of their own. Although it might have got its inspiration from and started off in 'Clair de Lune', it most emphatically did not want to stay or end there. A new challenge! ... this one was Johnnie's and, thanks to his powerful and sensitive musicianship, he rose magnificently to the occasion. We started the same way: he would begin playing and I would sit back, listen and wait. Johnnie was free to go in any direction he fancied. But once I had found my first image and started to develop it, to give it life, he had to listen very carefully and stay in sync with *my* story. The end result was that his musical scores for my scenarios were made up of bits and pieces of all the music he had in his repertoire, welded together by dramatic scales, arpeggios and original improvised passages.

These 'musical stories' as Johnnie and I called them, came out of lazy nothing-to-do Sunday afternoons when I had gone out to Salisbury Park ahead of my mom. But we were both so proud of what we had created that it wasn't long before they became full performances for the audience of our ever obliging and admiring mothers and occasional visitors. When this happened, the afternoon sessions became essential for the creation

35

and then the practising and polishing of the piece for the evening performance. With time they became very theatrical, the two of us incorporating in them any effect we could lay our hands on – candle light for romance, a completely dark lounge (Johnnie played remarkably well in the dark) for ghost stories, torch light on my contorted story-teller's face for the climactic moments, and so on. Our *pièce de resistance* was unquestionably the story of the Sacred Cobra of Rajastan. We had got together as usual one afternoon to prepare our show for the evening when our search for a story was interrupted by a commotion in the street outside. Somebody had spotted a snake in a bush and in typical South African fashion it was being stoned to death. By the time we joined the little crowd the drama was over, and the unfortunate reptile – as lifeless as a coil of boerewors – was the object of a lot of wary attention with the usual mutterings about 'gevaarlik' and 'giftig' and all the other prejudices of South African snake lore. Fortunately for us only the head had been smashed in. We both immediately saw its potential as the centrepiece of the evening's performance. We paid sixpence to the young boy who had first spotted it, scooped it into a box and carried it back indoors. Johnnie sat down at the piano. 'Where do we start?' he asked. I sank back into my favourite chair and, with a wonderful sense of authority as the story-teller answered, 'The East. Take me to The East.' Johnnie took up the cue splendidly and in no time, a stately caravan of long necked camels was marching out of a piece of music by Ketelby, bound for the bazaars of old Bombay where a mysterious snake charmer with a basket was waiting for me …

When our audience trooped into the lounge a few hours later a small coffee table had been positioned in the middle of the room, and on it was a mysterious looking basket. If their eyesight had been good enough in the deliberately dim lighting they would have also seen a length of black cotton leading from the basket up to the ceiling and then through a series of bent nails across to the piano – Johnnie's left hand was in charge of getting the snake to rise slowly out of the basket at the climax to the story while his right gave us the piping of the snake-charmer's flute. In addition to telling the story, I had to spotlight this dramatic moment with a torch. It was a triumph, both mothers letting out a genuine scream when the snake appeared. According to them my story-telling and Johnnie's playing had never been better. Even my Uncle Lou, who we had managed to coax into the lounge for this show, conceded that the effect had caught him by surprise, though he did mutter something about man's inhumanity to snakes which also had a right to live on the earth, as he went off to stir the pot of tripe and lights for his dogs.

I have come to believe that those sessions with Johnnie were the first formative experiences that led to my career as a dramatist. I am convinced that it was in that little lounge in Salisbury Park that I developed and shaped a dramatic imagination and forged what was to become a lifelong link between music and my writing process. It is a major connection in my life. To put it quite simply, I try to write plays with the same emotional dynamic, the same organisation of energy as there is in music. I am not just talking about the 'music of language', the poetic potential of the spoken word. I am very conscious of that marvellous potential in language, of creating a sort of music in our choice of words and the way we put them together, and I labour hard and happily at trying to craft that into my work. What I am really talking about now is the emotional event underneath that surface of words, and I am saying that I try to organise, control and direct that event in a way similar to the experience we have when we listen to music. The parallels between music and theatre as a whole, and not just my particular dramas, are very striking. Both have time, actual experienced time, as one of the major dimensions built into them. The conductor's baton goes up at eight o'clock and so does the curtain, and in both the concert hall and the theatre the audience falls silent. Half-an-hour, an hour, or two hours later it is all over. Beginning, middle and end. I call them 'time machines' because that is what they are designed to do, take you on an emotional and intellectual journey lasting a very specific period of time. Both have metronomes and clocks ticking away as pacemakers at the heart of their engines. One of the first things I do when settling down to write a new play is try literally to 'weigh' it in terms of 'time' – I try to determine what its ideal playing time should be. It is very important for a story-teller to make this assessment as accurately as possible. If your story needs an ideal ninety minutes for its telling and you try to stretch it out to one hundred and twenty or shrink it down to sixty, you'll be in trouble. Think of how diminished the impact would be if Beethoven got to that thrilling climax of the last movement of his ninth symphony five minutes too early. I can push the musical analogy to yet another level: Miss Helen's long speech to Dominee Marius Byleveld that climaxes Act 2 of *The Road to Mecca*. I don't know how many times I have heard it referred to by critics and audience alike as an 'aria', and I can remember very clearly how conscious I was when writing it of the need to organise the flow of thought and feeling in the same way for example that Mahler had done with that last magnificent 'Farewell' in his 'Song of the Earth' cycle. I don't think I have written a play without it having at least one extended aria in this fashion. It is also no coincidence that rehearsal room talk is about rhythm, tempo, pause, beat and crescendo as much as about the meaning of words and sentences.

I have an addictive personality, and a long time ago music became one of, if not the major dependency in my life. In his courageous and deeply moving account of his breakdown, William Styron writes about how he has always used a combination of music and alcohol to release his creativity. When I read what he had to say about this I recognised an important pattern in my own writing life. They came together so effortlessly – the carafe of red wine at the end of the day and a Bach unaccompanied cello suite – and the combination was so powerful, such an incredible lubricant of the cogs and wheels of the imagination! I always had to have pencil and paper at my side so that I could jot down the ideas that were released under their influence. This was particularly so late at night, when I would go to my desk for yet another carafe and more music, and when I would recklessly – and recklessness is essential to the process – brainstorm my way into images and scraps of dialogue that would be my springboard for the next day's writing. Right up until my fifty-second year I believed that my creativity was totally dependent on music and alcohol. In that year I finally faced up to the fact that I was an alcoholic, and decided to try and give up drinking even though a very insistent voice inside kept warning me that this would be the end of

Mother, from 'strong Afrikaner stock' and father, 'a perfect gentleman'

me as a writer. Heaven alone knows where I found the strength to ignore that warning, but I did and just as well. After a year of what can only be described as hell, during which I not only lost my impulse to write but my capacity for laughter, I returned slowly to life, to a new life in fact, and the biggest adventure I have ever had – sobriety. There have been four plays since that date and they have all enjoyed a measure of success. But don't think that has silenced that dangerous voice inside. Now it whispers: 'Ah, but just think how much better they would have been if you'd had a couple of whiskies inside.' Whatever the truth of that might be, does it mean I could now also live without music – because that addiction continues unabated – and still go on writing in some fashion or the other? I don't know, and I am not going to try to find out. It is a dependency of the soul which I think I share with most other human beings, and I believe it is meant to be that way.

Appropriately enough it is a little moment from my father's life that has provided me with the most beautiful and telling expression of this rich and mysterious dependency on music that we all share. It was an overheard snatch of dialogue between him and my mother in an adjoining room late one night. The stump of his amputated leg was causing him a lot of pain, and his groaning had become a rather strange sound. My mother asked him:

'Daddy, why are you chanting like a Jew?'
'Don't be silly. It's not Jewish. It's Persian.'
'That doesn't sound like Persian songs to me, Daddy.'
'You want to know what it is? My pain. I'm trying to make my pain sound nice.'

He sang in that fashion until the day he died.

Sadly for my relationship with Johnnie the time came when those Sunday sessions with him, important as they would eventually prove to be, were no longer my only adventures. Several other influences had come into my life and were contributing to the steady widening of my intellectual horizons. In so doing they began to free me of my emotional dependence on my cousin.

One of the most important of these was my discovery and exploration of the Port Elizabeth Public Library. I'll have more to say about it later on because it deserves very special mention. What it did for me in the world of literature, the 'wireless' did for me in the world of music. Where Johnnie had given me my first taste of classical music, it was the South African Broadcasting Corporation and its Tuesday night symphony concerts that now served up sumptuous banquets for me to feast on. I wonder if there has ever been a lover of classical music whose first love was not the Romantics? In my case that first love very quickly became a flaming and very long-burning passion. It was all consuming: Beethoven, Brahms, Schubert, Schumann, Tchaikovsky, Borodin, Rimsky-Korsakov, Chopin, and yet again Beethoven, Beethoven and still more Beethoven. Even as his music was sweeping me away with visions of a life of love and heroic action, Romain Rolland's *Jean Christophe* – the fictionalised biography of the life of a musical genius – was giving me my first understanding of the emotional turmoil and complex nature of creativity. The English essay I had to write for my final Matriculation examinations – the '… write five hundred words …' became a furiously scrawled couple of thousand – was an elaboration of the theory that if Beethoven had written a tenth symphony it would have taken the

40

synthesis of elements still further with the introduction of movement in addition to words and music. And four or five years later his music did in fact 'sweep me away' in every sense of the phrase. A totally unexpected and wild impulse had taken hold of my timid soul: abandon university and hitch-hike through Africa, see the world and become a writer. For weeks I agonised over the decision. Then one day I realised where I would find the courage I desperately needed in order to make the final plunge. I went down to the library of the College of Music in Rosebank and settled down in one of their audio booths with the master's Seventh Symphony. At the end of it I knew what I had to do. Two weeks later, with my mother's blessing, a change of clothing and ten tins of sardines in a haversack, I was standing on the side of the National Road outside Bellville with Perseus Adams the poet, thumbing passing cars.

Johnnie was not a part of these explorations. He had his own life: his work as a well-paid and qualified fitter and turner with the South African Railways, his musical ambition to lead a dance band of his own, and his still ongoing search – it would eventually be successful – for a young woman to share his life. Inevitably we began to drift apart and what made it all just a little bit sadder were the jealousies and judgements that crept into our relationship. On Johnnie's side I suspect there was a sense that with all my reading and talking about new composers and my plans for going to university I was becoming 'too big for my boots' ... and I'm sure he was right. My boasting about my book learning and music listening had turned a likeable Hally into a rather obnoxious, self-opinionated Athol. It got even worse once I was at university.

On my side the relationship turned sour when I began to suspect that Johnnie was deliberately not helping me in my attempts to master the piano for myself. I know I asked him for help, but it wasn't forthcoming. I also know now though that even if he had tried to help me it wouldn't have made that much difference. I was never cast to be a pianist in the same mould as he and my father.

There was no one specific incident that finally brought the relationship to an end. I wish there had been. My debt to it is so great it deserves something better than the slow withering and dying that was finally its fate. By the time I hitch-hiked down to Cape Town for my first year at university at the age of eighteen it was already dead. The break was made more permanent by the fact that Aunt Ann and Uncle Lou decided to sell their shop and move back to the Transvaal. Johnnie applied for a transfer and followed them.

All of that was forty-five years ago. Johnnie is still alive and enjoying good health, the father now of grown up children. He is living on his SAR pension in a small eastern Transvaal town where on Saturday nights he makes music at a local hotel. Neither of us ever made any attempt to reconnect with the other in the intervening years. I don't think this reflects on Johnnie in any way, he owes me little if anything at all; the debt in our relationship is all on my side. And it is a huge one. It invites the obvious and useless question: How different would my career as a writer have been if I hadn't found that second piano?

Looking back on the past I realise now that there have been quite a few other relationships over the years which in their own ways were every bit as important as the one with Johnnie, and which eventually suffered the same fate. What does this say about me? Is there an exploitative aspect to my nature? Do I enter into relationships that will be useful to me as a writer and then discard them when they have served their purpose? I live uneasily with the knowledge that the answer is probably 'yes'. All I can say in my defence is that it isn't something that I deliberately and consciously do. It is the instinctive nature of the Beast. The daemon of creativity is a selfish cannibal who can also be, when necessary, very cruel.

3

GARTH

I was writing at my desk one morning – I must have been about thirty at the time, which means that I would have been working on *The Bloodknot* – when my mother did something she normally tried her best to avoid: she came into the room and interrupted me. It was a timid intrusion, but as she explained she just had to tell me about the dream she had had the previous night. I put down my pen, she settled herself into a chair, and in hushed and awestruck tones, and in her wonderfully unique vocabulary of 'cock-rotted' English proceeded to recount it. She had dreamt, she said, that she was helping Jesus carry his cross to his crucifixion. According to her there were 'thousands and thousands of people' and they were going up a very steep hill which somehow seemed vaguely familiar. Her description of the two of them labouring under their burden – their groans of despair, their heavy breathing, their sweat, the crown of thorns on Jesus's head – was very specific and graphic. Then, about half way up the hill, she discovered why it all seemed so familiar: chancing to look to one side she saw a bright orange signboard with plain no frills white lettering hanging out over the pavement:

JUBILEE RESIDENTIAL HOTEL
SINGLES AND DOUBLES – FULL BOARD
Prop: H.D.L. Fugard.

Golgotha was at the top of Constitution Hill in Port Elizabeth!

It is by any standards a very steep hill, and I am sure there were many times when it felt like her personal Via Dolorosa as she trudged up it to that signboard, which was about a third of the way up. We had moved

Birthday party at the Jubilee Residential Hotel with all the boarders in attendance. Birthday girl Glenda is flanked by her parents

into the Jubilee Residential Hotel after the death of my paternal grandmother had brought to an end our comfortable and protected years in quiet and very respectable Clevedon Road and forced us out into the big world. Hardly a stone's throw away, at the bottom of the Hill, was Main Street, then Port Elizabeth's principal business and shopping centre. It was 1940 and I was eight years old at the time.

If I remember correctly, there were sixteen rooms, singles and doubles, and all furnished with only the bare essentials: bed, dressing table, wardrobe, washstand with enamel jug, basin and potty, and a chair. I can't remember any pictures on the walls of those dark little rooms. Our 'permanent' boarders obviously did their best to give their rooms a bit of character, but for the rest they were archetypal transit spaces – the sagging mattress and cigarette burns on the furniture being the only clues to the men and women who had passed through them. During our six years in the hotel I managed to sleep in thirteen of the rooms. I can remember very clearly how much I regretted the three that had eluded me when we finally sold up and left in 1946. It felt as if I had failed to complete a major mission in my life.

In my play *Master Harold ... and the Boys*, this is how Hally remembers the Jubilee:

HALLY: Which meant I got another rowing for hanging around the 'servants quarters'. I think I spent more time in there with you chaps than anywhere else in that dump. And do you blame me? Nothing but bloody misery wherever you went. Somebody was always complaining about the food or my mother was having a fight with Micky Nash because she'd caught her with a Petty Officer in her room. Maud Meiring was another one. Remember those two? They were prostitutes you know. Soldiers and sailors from the troopships. Bottom fell out of the business when the war ended. God, the flotsam and jetsam that life washed up on our shores! No joking, if it wasn't for your room I would have been the first certified ten-year-old in medical history. Ja, the memories are coming back now. Walking home from school and thinking: What can I do this afternoon? Try out a few ideas but sooner or later I'd end up in there with you fellows. I bet you I could still find my way to your room with my eyes closed.

[He does exactly that]

Down the corridor ... telephone on the right which my mom keeps locked because somebody is using it on the sly and not paying ... past the kitchen and unappetising cooking smells ... around the corner into the backyard, hold my breath again because there are more smells coming when I pass your lavatory, then into that little passageway, first door on the right and into your room.

How's that?

SAM: Good. But as usual you forgot to knock.

Hally is being a little unfair. Those years in the old Jubilee were not as bad as he makes out. 'Boring' they most certainly were not. In fact as regards people and incidents, the Jubilee was far and away the most exciting of the four homes of my youth. To start with, all it needed as you stepped out of the front door, was a left turn and then a hop and a skip downhill and you were slap in the middle of Main Street – and in those years, 1940 to 1946, it was a genuine *main* street – the hub of 'good old PE' … we Port Elizabethans have no problems with the acronym. At one end of it was the City Hall, white, square and as solid as the wedding cakes my mother baked and decorated as a sideline, and at the other – it runs due North – beckoning me through all of my childhood and youth, was Africa.

The world couldn't have been any wider than that. I had a choice of no fewer than five cinemas in the immediate neighbourhood – The Grand, Astra, Metro, Opera and Popular, the latter being one of those wonderful old 'bio-cafés' where you sipped a green cooldrink while watching Gene Autry or the Lone Ranger galloping after rustlers and stage-coach robbers. Whenever I had the price of a ticket I would dash around to each in turn to see what was showing before making my choice. Also only minutes away from the hotel were the Port Elizabeth Public Library, the Willowtree Ice-cream Parlour and the Donkin Reserve – a large, open public space with a lighthouse in the middle, and a few stands of scraggly, gnarled pines. This was my personal playground; it was here that I came to hide away from my mom whenever I had done anything really wicked, and it was here that I flew kites with Sam, and where with my cousin Garth I had one of the most decisive experiences of my childhood.

But for all the bustle of its crowded pavements and its dazzling shop windows, when it came to real excitement Main Street couldn't compete with its major tributary at the City Hall end – notorious Jetty Street. It is a name that still resonates for me with rich undertones of violence and sin. At the bottom of it, and flanking the Campanile – our well-known monument to the 1820 Settlers – were the railway station and dock gates. Although it was only a few blocks long, Jetty Street was a world unto itself of brawls and beggars, coloured fishermen from the line boats and trawlers, drunken sailors off the warships berthed beyond the dock gates, and inevitably, our ladies-of-the-night. The high point of my brief journalistic career in the city fifteen years later was a front page exposé in the *Evening Post* headlined 'Vice rackets boom in the Friendly City'. I had used my recently acquired experience as a sailor to get into the dagga dens and brothels. The story led to my first brush with the South

Primary schoolboy, 'innocent Hally'

African Police, who called me in for questioning and tried to get me to divulge names and addresses. I was already an accomplished liar by then so I had no difficulty in covering my tracks and protecting my informants. In 1940, however, it was still a wide-eyed and innocent Hally who hung around in the shadows of Jetty Street spying on the rough and raw life coursing along its pavements.

Looking back now I am amazed at how many of the formative experiences of my childhood are crowded into those six years. Among the major ones was unquestionably my discovery of the beautiful Port Elizabeth Public Library situated, with an appropriate symbolism in terms of the choices to be made in life, opposite the entrance to Jetty Street. I wish I could remember who it was who first introduced me to its hushed and civilised atmosphere, because I can't believe I had the temerity to walk into it of my own accord. I have never had the sort of 'guts' to change my luck by walking into places and situations where I might not be welcome. To whoever it was, and my guess is that it was my dad, I owe one of the big debts of my life. I read recently that inscribed above the library of Pharoah Rameses II were the words: 'The Place of the

47

Cure of the Soul'. At the age of eight my soul didn't as yet need much curing in the medical sense, but in the secondary one of preserving something for future use, it certainly got a very good literary salting in those reading rooms.

My first passion was the American Wild West and I proceeded to hunt down and devour every western I could lay my hands on. One name still leaps to mind: William 'Colt' McDonald, my favourite author. My subscription entitled me to two books, and for an extra sixpence I could have a third. That was the rate at which I devoured them – three a week. A few years ago I had a very vivid and happy recall of those hours of feverish reading when I went out to Southern California for the first time to direct one of my plays. Those long forgotten adventures with posses and sheriffs and gun-slingers, cowboys in batwing chaps and pretty schoolmarms in gingham dresses came back to me vividly as I used my free time to drive around the American South West – the setting of many of the stories. This was the world I had had to create imaginatively for myself, using the clues on the printed page and images from the black and white 'cowboy pictures' that flickered on the screens of the bioscopes. There was a genuine thrill of recognition when I saw the name of my first real-life ranch – the Bar-E – on a drive into the Anza Borrego Desert. And then all the other names that worked so powerfully and indelibly on my young imagination – Wells Fargo, Pony Express, Dodge City, Wyoming, Arizona, gulch, arroyo – they were all around me, even in downtown San Diego. But at the rate of three and sometimes four books a week, I was soon scraping the bottom of the western barrel. Moderation has always eluded me; I still eat my food as if I hadn't had a square meal for days.

From western adventure I turned to African adventure, a phase that started off with the Tarzan romances of Edgar Rice Burroughs, then broadened out to include Rider Haggard, John Buchan and anything else I could find that was written in that florid romantic idiom. It wasn't long however before this line of reading led me away from the main ground floor reading room to the first gallery where the African Natural History section was located. Africa was, after all, my own world, and because of that it wasn't fiction I wanted but the real thing. This was the beginning of a lifelong passion for the flora and fauna of the continent. Once I had got into these upper galleries and started exploring the world of serious fiction, the real adventure began. I can't remember any more in what order they came, but there was Dumas, Hugo and eventually Zola and Flaubert as well; those monumental Russians – Tolstoy, Dostoevsky (pronounced Dostoofski) and Turgenev – and then one day, relegated to dust and oblivion in an unlit little corridor right up on the top gallery, an unknown American author called William Faulkner. What on earth prompted me to take out that first novel I'll never know. And what on earth made me persist in my attempt to read it, because it was really heavy going, I also don't know. And then finally, after all of that, why on earth did I go on to take out a second novel by this man who seemed determined to make life as difficult as possible for the reader? But take it out I did, and slowly, laborious page by laborious page, I mastered the code of Faulkner's time and place. It was a profound and inspirational lesson to me as a writer, even though I didn't know it at the time. More than anybody else I was to read it was Faulkner who gave me the courage to embrace, uncompromisingly, my identity as a regional writer. In my early formative years as a playwright, when most of the critics were urging me to stop addressing myself so specifically to fellow South Africans and to think of the wider English speaking audience, it was his example that kept me passionately rooted in my 'time and place'. A few years later it would again be American literature, through the work of Eugene O'Neill, Tennessee Williams, Arthur Miller and Clifford Odets, that would provide me with my first lessons in the craft of play writing.

But all of that was still in the future as I prowled those galleries with their beautiful wrought iron railings, looking down with disdain on the common folk grubbing around for cheap thrillers and love stories on the ground floor. Initially the librarians – a very superior 'English spoken the way it ought to be' bunch of women – viewed with a measure of mild distaste the little scruff off the streets who had suddenly become a regular, and who was seen wandering all over the place instead of staying in the Juvenile Reading Room where he belonged. Their suspicions about me being up to no good were finally confirmed when it was discovered that I was the culprit responsible for taking books off the shelves where they belonged and hiding them behind other less frequented shelves – the theological section being my favourite. I was eventually caught red-handed by one of these well-elocuted dragons. I admitted my guilt, and explained that I did it because of the frequent frustration at finding that somebody had taken out a book I had planned to read next. My excuse was to no avail. I was summarily marched into the office of the head librarian, a man. He was a lot more sympathetic and questioned me about my reading and interest in books. At the end of the interview he instructed the dragon who was hovering in the background, hoping no doubt to see my subscription cancelled, to set aside a space behind the counter where I would be allowed to keep three books on reserve for myself.

❏   ❏   ❏

There was one colossal reality that over-rode everything else in giving this period its unique and never-to-be-forgotten character: The War. These were the years of the Second World War. The consequences of that cataclysmic event were not limited to the headlines and front page stories of desert battles and torpedoed ships in the *Eastern Province Herald* and the *Evening Post*. They were felt in very real and immediate terms by the ordinary men, women and children on the pavements of Main Street. Many of my school mates sitting with me in the classrooms of the Albert Jackson Primary School had brothers, fathers and uncles, and even a few sisters with 'the boys up North'. I felt so left out of this club that I ended up inventing a fictitious First World War record for my dad, claiming that he had lost his leg in the Battle of the Somme – I never missed out in my youth on a chance to scrounge a bit of pity. In the cinemas we all jumped to our feet with patriotic fervour at the end of the showing when God Save the King was played and the picture of George VI was flashed on the screen. I can also still remember marvelling at the heavy and eerie quiet that settled on Main Street during the first weeks of the Normandy invasion, when the City Hall clock struck noon and we all paused in our tracks to observe a minute of silence. It was also in Main Street, in one of the large display windows of the OK Bazaars to be precise, that the war lost its simple 'Good guy, bad guy' and 'Bang you're dead' scenario and became a nightmare dreamt up by a madman. The object of our silent, open-mouthed, head-shaking disbelief as we congregated in front of that display window was an exhibition of photographs of the living skeletons and mountains of dead bodies in mass graves and gas chambers that were discovered when two of Hitler's extermination camps, Belsen and Buchenwald, were liberated. I stumbled on them by accident during one of my sorties into Main Street, pushing my way rudely to the front of the crowd to see what everybody was whispering about. I think there are moments in the living of a life that are so startling in their impact and penetration of your psyche that you never leave them. This was one of them for me. A part of me is still standing in front of that large glass showcase, so frightened by what I saw that I wanted to run home to the safety of my mother's arms and warm body, but unable to leave. I have gone back to that moment from time to time in my life, and I always find myself still standing there.

With its proximity to the railway station and dock gates the Jubilee was a perfect setting for wartime dramas. These ranged from passionate weekend romances between our 'single' ladies and the homesick and lovelorn soldiers and sailors who passed through town, to the discovery that one of our boarders – an Afrikaner woman and a Nazi sympathiser ('she had Hitler on the wall,' according to my mother) – was spying for the Germans. There was talk that she was actually caught radioing ship movements to German subs, but I have no recollection of the drama getting that serious. Years afterwards my mother always boasted very proudly that she personally, with a carving knife from the kitchen, had slashed the motor-car tyres of the woman's Ossewa Brandwag boyfriend.

Even the old Jubilee itself picked up a moment of glory when a well-aimed German torpedo resulted in a group of Free French sailors being billeted with us. One of them had been the chef of a well-known, Michelin-rated Marseilles restaurant before the war. My mother, with a passion for all things French thanks to Charles Boyer, opened her heart and arms to a fellow cook and caterer, and in no time he was installed in the kitchen and in charge of the pots and pans on the big gas range. For a couple of weeks the Jubilee Residential Hotel boasted a cordon bleu menu on the twelve tables in its dining room. Sad to say, our boarders failed to appreciate their good fortune. After a few weeks of grumbles and mutterings and suspicious sniffings of strange dishes with unpronouncable French names, my mother was told by a deputation of our 'permanents' that they preferred the old menu of tomato bredies and cabinet puddings. She was outraged, but a show-down was averted when a passing troop ship took the Frenchmen on board.

As it turned out though, strict rationing of basic foodstuffs made it anything but easy for my mother to serve up the bredies and puddings, and she was forced into a few minor breaches of the rationing regulations in order to keep her boarders satisfied. One of these involved a weekly sunset car ride to buy black market meat from a butcher in the little rural community of Kleinskool. Although that drive of about fifteen miles each way was through some of the poorest areas of Port Elizabeth, it has remained one of the indelible and special memories of my childhood. As I sat there in the front seat next to my mom, it stirred up feelings which would eventually spill over into my writing. At that hour the Uitenhage mountains ahead of us were bathed in a magical afterglow. With all of Africa lying behind them, they beckoned to me in a way I would one day find irresistible. This was the first time I had a sense of Africa as an epic adventure – a vision which finally found its expression in the mouth of my beloved Mr M in *My Children! My Africa!* But those distant mountains, with their alluringly vague promise of adventure in strange and exotic worlds weren't the only images at work on me. Flashing by on the side of the road, right under the nose pressed against the window of the old Ford, were glimpses of a totally different world from the comfortable, middle class white one I knew. Candlelit interiors of humble corrugated iron and mud dwellings; barefoot ragged children still at play in the half light outside the glowing doorways; the pious little Kleinskool Church with its bell suspended between two poles, the ground around it tramped as hard as concrete by Sunday congregations; goats and oxen straggling out of the dense prickly pear bush and heading for kraals as night settled in … these were my first tantalising glimpses of a world I would one day claim as my special territory as a writer. By the time we drove back into town, the boot loaded up with a couple of legs of lamb and an assortment of other cuts, together with a few kidneys for my dad, it was already dark and I was left savouring the delicious bittersweet feelings with which that drive always left me … feelings which will surge as the generative energy of my writing.

❑   ❑   ❑

Saturday was the high point in Main Street's weekly cycle. In the morning it was mostly business and bargains that had the pavements crowded with shoppers and hawkers, while for us kids there was the attraction of special children's shows at the bios. After an afternoon lull, it came to life again in the evening when grown-up Port Elizabeth took time off to have a little bit of fun. By and large this consisted of getting dressed up to promenade and window shop along the brightly lit frontages of the department stores – the OK Bazaars, Woolworths, Ackermans, Kolnicks and Garlicks – or to queue up for a seat in one of the cinemas. Other than an evening of boozing in one of the hotel lounges or, for the tame souls, a banana split in a milk bar, there really wasn't anything else going by way of a good time in the heart of 'The Friendly City'. For various reasons parental supervision of our free time was very lax, so I invariably ended up in those Saturday night crowds, prowling the pavements in search of adventure, and of course never finding it. It always seemed such a real possibility though. Surely something extraordinary would come out of that crowd of eager, noisy people and the general atmosphere of excitement? The expectation was further heightened if there happened to be a troop or battleship in port. Then the crowd on the pavements would even spill out into the street with the influx of khaki and navy blue uniforms who were trying every bit as hard as Hally to have a Saturday night adventure. Ironically enough it was my mother who came the nearest to providing it for them. She tried, with varying degrees of success, to supplement the family income by organising what a few dozen hurriedly printed posters euphemistically described as a 'Hospitality Dance'. For this she hired the cavernous Feather Market Hall and a New Brighton dance band and then threw open the doors to the Limeys, Yanks, Aussies, Kiwis, Frogs or whatever other nationality had dropped anchor in the harbour. For the

53

'single ladies' of the Jubilee and related establishments it was an opportunity to make a real killing. That was when you raised your sights above the privates, ratings and petty officers, and aimed at something with gold braid on its cap, brass pips on its shoulder tab and, best of all, an American drawl in its mouth. As Mickey Nash, one of the 'single ladies' used to say to me in her wonderful attempt at a Southern accent: 'Those Yanks are well paid, honey'.

My brother and I were roped in to do our share on these occasions. Royal was installed at one end of the dance floor with a bottle opener, a pocket full of small change, and a few dozen cases of cooldrinks – the licence prohibited the sale of alcoholic beverages – while I went into the ticket booth, standing on an empty cooldrink box in a vain attempt to add a few inches of authority to my height. Although I was the best in the family when it came to arithmetic, I think the real reason for my being put in charge of ticket sales was so that my mother could indulge her passionate love of dancing. She always wore a long evening dress to these dances, and by being in the ticket box I freed her to waltz, tango, Paul Jones and foxtrot the night away. I can't really say I enjoyed myself all that much. On the one hand, knowing how desperate the family's finances usually were it gave me an avaricious pleasure to see the ten shilling and one pound notes piling up in the cashbox, but on the other, I absolutely hated having to deal with the drunk sailors and soldiers who hung around and tried to get in for half price or less after the dance had been under way for an hour or so. My sister eventually also put in an appearance at these dances. My mother had the bright idea that Glenda and I should entertain the crowd with an interlude of ballroom dancing – we had both taken lessons and were considered quite good. On one occasion we tried out something very different. I had seen a Parisian 'apache' dance in a movie and, inspired by it, I took Glenda out onto the dance floor and threw her around wildly for about five minutes. It was a huge success.

'Hospitality' always ended precisely on the stroke of midnight – the Sunday Observance laws were very strictly enforced – and then came the best part of the evening as far as I was concerned. After cashing up in the ticket booth, and regardless of whether it had been a good or a bad

PORT ELIZABETH, CAPE PROVINCE

GARLICKS

THE DEPARTMENT STORE

PHONE   TELEGRAMS   P.O.BOX
2222   Garlicks, Port Elizabeth   317

1st March 1944

Miss & Master Fugard,
  c/o Jubilee Boarding House,
   Constitution Hill,
    Port Elizabeth.

<u>MARCO ASSOCIATION</u>

Dear Miss & Master Fugard,
        Please accept our hearty thanks for
your contribution towards making our Social
Evening in the Feather Market on Tuesday night
such an outstanding success. You really put up
a fine show, that everybody enjoyed and greatly
appreciated.
        We hope, as a result of our effort
to send a good donation to the Red Cross Prisoner
of War Fund.
        Congratulations and a big Thank You.

      Yours faithfully,
      Hon. Secretary.

H. Croft

night, we bundled into the old Ford and drove down to Strand Street for a midnight snack at Uncle Sam's 'Cave de-move-on' … a trailer food stand that served hot dogs and hamburgers and very sweet coffee to Port Elizabeth's night owls.

As faithful and diligent as I always was in my search for that illusive Saturday night adventure, I never found it. When the City Hall clock chimed ten I was usually trailing my way dispiritedly back to the Jubilee. This sad state of affairs was made even more depressing by the prospect of what lay immediately ahead – the Sabbath! Those years in Constitution Hill have left me with a lifelong and morbid fascination with desolate and empty Sunday streets. To be accurate though, Sunday morning and afternoon weren't all that bad. If you had the price of a tram ticket you could always ride the big double-decker out to Humewood and spend the day on the beach. Even if you didn't have the money, it wasn't all that long a walk to the first stretch of sand and sea which we used to call S-bend until it was tarted up for the Royal Visit in 1948 after which it changed its name to King's Beach. It was the Sunday nights that did it to me. Standing at the bottom of Constitution Hill and looking to the left and right along the deserted length of Main Street you knew, with a sinking heart and total certainty you *just knew*, that there was no adventure to be found on those pavements. Nothing was open along the entire length of the street, not even my favourite little hole-in-the-wall Indian fruit shop where I used to buy sweets and cooldrinks. The sense of a world abandoned was heightened by the intermittent arrival and departure of empty buses to and from the suburbs, the Circle tram clanging past without any passengers, and the occasional lost soul drifting along the pavements as purposelessly as a piece of newspaper being waltzed around by the wind. In fact, as the saying goes, they might just as well have rolled up those pavements and put them away until Monday.

This bleak Sunday scenario was always brought to an appropriately doleful conclusion by a circle of Salvation Army singers and musicians at the bottom of Donkin Street, one street along from the Jubilee. The music was dreadful and the Bible reading and preaching just another variation of what had bored me to distraction in Sunday School earlier in the day. In spite of that I was fascinated by them. As I saw it, it took real courage to dress up in that outfit and stand there in the middle of the world playing that dreadful music and singing those tuneless hymns. Another reason for hanging around was the march to 'Headquarters' at the end of the service. That was where the homeless were provided with a meal and a free bed for the night. We all marched in time to the beat of a big bass drum which one of the soldiers carried suspended on his chest. I enjoyed the march very much, but that was as far as my commitment to God's yeomanry went. When we reached Headquarters I turned away and ran back to the Jubilee.

It is obvious to me now that in exploring the life of that little world centred on the Jubilee, I was actually scouting out yet another province of my future territory as a writer. It was a world of so-called 'ordinary people', though that is not the adjective I would use to describe the lives I studied on the pavements of Main Street and in the dark little rooms of the Jubilee, and which gave me my understanding of words like courage and hope and despair. Over the years I have readily identified myself as a regional writer. In elaborating on my unhesitating and happy acceptance of that label – as compared with my impatience at being pigeon-holed as a 'political playwright' – I always use a little illustration that remains as true of myself and my work today as it was fifteen or twenty years ago when I came out with it for the first time. It goes something like this: put me on a street corner of New York, or London, or Toronto, or Amsterdam – to name just a few foreign cities that I know reasonably well – and I am at a complete loss to make any real sense of the tide of humanity flowing past me on the pavement. I just can't 'read' it and conjecture meaningfully about any of the faces I happen to focus on. But put me on a street corner in Port Elizabeth and it is a completely different matter. That young African woman with a shopping bag for example, hurrying desperately down Russel Road in the late afternoon, and obviously headed for the township bus terminus in Strand Street … I know all the possible white families whose house she could have cleaned that day, and if you wanted it, I could also itemise for you the pile of dirty washing that kept her bent over a zinc tub in the backyard all afternoon long; I also know the little two-roomed matchbox in KwaZakhele township which she calls home and where an unemployed and bitter husband and small children are waiting to eat the leftovers from the white family's table which she has got carefully wrapped up in that plastic shopping bag; I can also eavesdrop on the conversation of husband and wife later that night when the children are asleep and they talk about the next day's survival and dream about a better future. In like fashion, standing on that PE street corner I can put together a plausible scenario for any of the faces – young and old, male and female, black and white, coloured and Indian – that I happen to focus on. To repeat my stock phrase: I have mastered the code of one place and time; it is the Eastern Cape and the time is all of the life that started with that little boy scurrying around the streets of Port Elizabeth like one of the cockroaches that swarm under their lampposts at night. There is a poem by Cavafy that perfectly expresses the truth of my relationship to this magnificently 'ordinary' world that I called home for so long.

The City

You said: 'I'll go to another land, go to another sea.
Another city shall be found better than this.
All I have ever tried to do was doomed to fail, and my heart
is like a body dead and buried.
For how long will my thoughts stay in this state of
desolation?
Wherever I turn my eyes, no matter where I look,
I see the black ruins of my life here,
where I have spent so many years and wasted and ruined them.'

You will not find new places, you will not find other seas.
The city will follow you. And you will grow old in the same
streets, in the same neighbourhoods;
in these same houses your hair will grow white.
It is always this city that you will reach. Do not hope that
you will ever get anywhere else;
for you there is no ship, no road.
As you have ruined your life here in this small corner, so you
have ruined it in the whole world.

There was a moment in my early thirties when I railed against 'my city' in the same fashion. A strange misadventure in Zambia where I had been directing a production of Brecht's *Caucasian Chalk Circle* had ended with me being thrown out of the country and flying off to New York to see and enjoy my first overseas triumph – the now famous first American production of *The Blood Knot* with James Earl Jones and JD Cannon. It was indeed, and from everybody – actors, director, designers – an incredible piece of work, and for me an incredibly heady experience. What could be a better introduction to that extraordinary city than to be the author of a play singled out by the *New York Times* critic as 'best of the season'. Personal circumstances however forced a hurried return to

58

PE cutting short the wonderful time I was having in New York – I was living in the producer's personal suite in the Plaza Hotel when the telegram arrived calling me home. I did so with a heart full of anger and resentment. 'Dear old PE' seemed so drab and ugly and uninteresting after the bright lights and glamour of a New York success. Walking down Jetty Street one night shortly after my return, I passed a drunk bleary-eyed coloured woman, her face swollen and bruised from recent beatings. The top of her dress was torn open, revealing a pair of flabby breasts. In an instant, in all of her ugliness, she became a symbol of the world that had claimed me. An inner voice spoke out in protest: 'And I must love you?' In an instant another voice replied simply: 'Yes. You must love her. She is all you've got, all you will ever have.' Those were my orders. I have tried to obey them.

But all of that lay in the future. Back in those war years I was kept very busy studying the fascinating assortment of individuals passing through the rooms of the boarding house. I spied and eavesdropped on them at every opportunity and in every possible way: through keyholes and chinks in the curtains, with glass tumblers pressed against the wall so that I could hear conversations in adjoining rooms, and once, using my reflection in the mirror, I made a real attempt at mastering the art of lip reading so that I could follow conversations at a distance. From mysterious overnighters who drifted up from Main Street suitcase in hand for 'Bed and Breakfast' and were never seen again, to the 'permanents' who behaved as if they owned the joint, they were male and female, old and young, English and Afrikaans, loaded with 'moola' or down and out, prim and proper or wild and wicked – you name it and at some point or other it had bedded down in a room at the Jubilee. There can be no question though, that in this motley parade of humanity the single most disturbing and challenging presence was unquestionably that of 'Cousin Garth', arriving always unannounced from God alone knows where with the rank odour of a sweating, unwashed body and a laugh that has haunted me all my life.

❏　❏　❏

The 'wicked Fugards'
Uncle Garth, Aunt Dulcie and Cousin Garth

We were frightened of him, all of us – mother, father and the three children. I don't know how the snob Fugards reacted to him, but in whatever way they did you can be certain their feelings were as complex and strong as ours. It just wasn't possible to be lukewarm about Cousin Garth and his branch of the family. There were three of them – Uncle Garth senior, my Aunt Dulcie, and their only child, Cousin Garth. Aunt Dulcie was quite simply an angel – a fascinating example of a gentle and refined woman falling passionately in love with a wild and violent man. Life and literature are full of examples of that mysterious attraction of opposites. In Aunt Dulcie's case it was given a further twist by the fact that her one and only child turned out to be every bit as unpredictable and disturbed as his father. Among the odds and ends of Cousin Garth's 'personal possessions' that I inherited after his death a few years ago, was a memento of his mother's childhood: a bronze school medal in a small velvet-lined box. It was from the Worcestershire County Council for unbroken school attendance from 1900 to 1907. Depending on how you looked at it, that capacity for constant and earnest effort was either her blessing or her curse. Her devotion and loyalty to the two men she loved, husband and son, both of whom were to give her great joy and also cause her great grief, was as complete and unwavering through all of her adult life as those eight years at a school desk had been in her youth. If I have one regret now as regards lost opportunities with family members, it is in relation to Aunt Dulcie. I wish I had taken the chance when they were there, and got to know her better, but I'm ashamed to say I wasted them.

As for Uncle Garth ... the reality is so huge, it is hard to know where to begin. The following I know to be fact: sailor (merchant marine), soldier (First World War, wounded in action), professional boxer, civil engineer (road and bridge builder), Rhodesian farmer and breeder of prize-winning ridgebacks, alcoholic, and finally blind and broke, looked after by Aunt Dulcie in a little cottage somewhere on the Cape Peninsula where he died. What I am not certain about, though my dad passed on these stories to me as fact, is that in America he carried a gun for Dutch Schultz during the prohibition, that as a member of a silk and carpet caravan he had walked across the Gobi desert, and that at one point during his years as a sailor his ship had docked in PE harbour with him in chains and facing charges for having assaulted an officer. According to my dad's story my grandmother paid a huge bribe to the captain to have him unshackled and signed off. What I find surprising though is that for all the extravagance of both the hard facts and possible fictions about this remarkable man, I do not have a very clear memory of him. Apart from a face which I vaguely remember when I look at family photographs, all that really comes back to me from those years is a very hearty voice. Much more vivid is my memory of the excitement in our family when he and Aunt Dulcie came down from Rhodesia to visit. At that time he was a very successful tobacco farmer and the two of them swept into our lives with an aura of affluence and style. In all fairness to my uncle, I should also say I can't ever remember him importuning my family in the way that his son eventually did. He was too proud for that, as was Aunt Dulcie. Even in his final years, when the two of them were really having a hard time trying to make ends meet, there was never any appeal for help.

Cousin Garth on the other hand *was* trouble – and we all knew it! The spasm of panic that passed through the family whenever the word came through that 'young Garth' was in town and headed our way was based, like his father's reputation, on a lurid mix of fact and fiction, of dark unmentionable secrets and just plain prejudice. To start with my mother was convinced that he was a thief and that he pilfered from the family treasury – her handbag – whenever her back was turned. There might have been some truth in this, though I must also say that my mother's paranoia about the money she worked so hard to earn, made just about everybody, family members included, and there were no exceptions – potentially suspect on this score. But knowing Garth as I do now, I could quite easily see him sneaking a quid or two out of my mother's handbag when he got a chance. Either way, when he put in one of his unexpected appearances she wasted no time in hauling out the formidable bunch of keys she carried between her ample breasts and locking away in cupboards and wardrobes anything of value that might tempt the light-fingered Garth. They were both fairly thick-skinned about all of this. I can remember one occasion in my parents' bedroom in the boarding house when I watched mortified as my mother went about this precautionary measure while chatting amiably to Garth who had just arrived and was lounging in a chair. I can't believe he didn't know what she was doing. It was perfectly obvious to me because she wasn't making the slightest attempt to disguise the operation. Her theory about him and the waste of his life as we all saw it, was that he was waiting for his father to die so that he could inherit the £500 that our grandmother had left in trust for each of her grandchildren. That he was waiting for it I don't doubt, but there were much deeper and darker reasons for his inability to achieve that great middle-class ambition – settling down and leading a normal life.

My father's anxieties about his nephew on the other hand were very obviously a hangover from his own youth when Garth senior had been the family terror. As far as he was concerned it was a case of a 'chip off the old block'. 'Like father like son' was another phrase I heard from him many times when young Garth had 'done it again'. There is a hidden irony in his use of these tired old saws, because in thinking about it now I suspect that there was a more deep-seated and personal fear involved, not so much of the younger man personally, but of what his disturbed behaviour represented. I'm thinking here about the thread of addiction that I can see running through the two generations of Fugard men … my father and Uncle Garth, Cousin Garth and myself …

It was certainly no fiction that Cousin Garth seemed incapable of settling down. Not that he was ever without that laudable intention. On the contrary it was usually the first thing we heard after he had greeted 'Aunty Betty' and 'Uncle Harold'. The pattern never varied: he would arrive in town travel stained and weary, announce to my sceptical parents his determination to turn over a new leaf and then ask them if they would 'billet' one of 'life's veterans' (he was twenty-five years old) until he had 'regrouped his forces' – and while they were about it a few bob in his pocket for 'fags and fighting rations' would be greatly appreciated as well. He had recently been discharged, on medical grounds, from the army, and his conversation was liberally peppered with military expressions. Having secured his billet and fighting rations he would then scan the 'situations vacant' column of the *Herald* for a likely looking 'situation' – usually something of a very basic clerical nature; I think Garth knew a little about bookkeeping. It is not surprising that he usually landed what he went after – Cousin Garth could turn on a lot of charm and look very responsible and ready for 'settling down' when he wanted to. Once he had landed the job we could rely on at least a few weeks of relative peace, quiet and sobriety. On one occasion it even stretched into a couple of months which prompted my mother to remark that it looked as if 'Garthie has finally pulled himself together … thank God!' Sadly, that was not the case. Those few months of middle-class sanity ended as all the others had done – in a huge binge, with Garth rolling up drunk for work and being fired. He never hung around once

63

that happened. We'd wake up one morning and, with a concerted sigh of relief, discover him gone.

In the eyes of us children there was an aura of mystery about our disturbed and disturbing cousin. His arrival in town was always followed by a veiled warning from our parents to be careful with him. When I tried to nail them down with childhood's inevitable 'Why?' all I got was that he wasn't to be trusted and 'don't ask any more questions'. My brother and sister succeeded I think in keeping him at arm's length, but I was fascinated by him, drawn to him in the same way as I am to the edges of cliffs or high balconies, even though I have a terrible fear of heights.

My earliest memory of Garth is, appropriately enough, immediately after one of those 'out of the blue' arrivals at the Jubilee. I was called to my mother's bedroom where I found my cousin and a very obviously disconcerted 'Aunty Betty' who gave me a key to one of the small back rooms and told me to show Cousin Garth where he could 'spend a few nights'. She was wasting her time dropping hints like that. To use one of her own favourite expressions, they 'rolled off his back like duck's water'. Garth's arrivals and departures were timed to his own irrational schedule. I led him up stairs and along the passageway to a dark, windowless little room, and that is where my memory is as clear as if it had only happened yesterday … sitting on the bed, watching and listening with total fascination while he unpacked and settled in. I was his audience and like a true Fugard, he found a good performance for the occasion.

To start with, it really is a gross exaggeration to describe as 'unpacking' what happened after he'd opened a battered and travel weary little suitcase. All that came out of it were a few miserable, and as far as I could tell, unwashed items of underclothing, an already half empty bottle of brandy and finally, held up for my examination with a great flourish of pride, a Salvation Army uniform and collection box. He described it variously as his camouflage, his 'last resort outfit', his survival kit and his beggar's rags. He made recourse to it only when all his other stratagems for keeping body and soul together had failed. When that was the case he would put it on and go from house to house soliciting contributions '… for the needy, the homeless and the hungry' from all the good

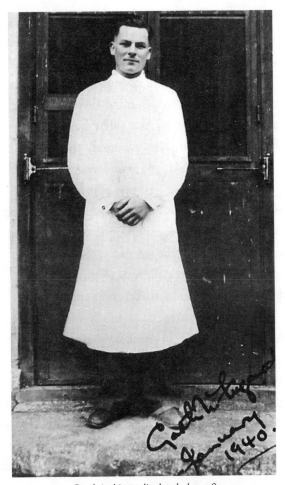

Garth in his medical orderly outfit

Christians who opened their front doors to his polite and deferential knock. A tumbler of brandy and water in hand he explained to me that, strictly speaking he wasn't really doing anything wrong. He was, as it were, only taking a short cut in the charitable process by going directly to the source. All he had in fact done was eliminate the middle man. And the uniform? No, that was not a deception. He was, he assured me, a member of God's yeomanry and to prove this he interrupted the flow of his monologue with a hymn sung in his fine tenor voice. He did so with such conviction that I could almost hear the Salvation Army Band at the bottom of Donkin Street accompanying him. He sang it through to the last bar in spite of loud banging on the wall from the boarder next door. With the uniform carefully hung up in the wardrobe, ready for use should the need arise, he replenished his glass, settled down in a chair and moved on to other matters. I was enthralled. He was a compulsive talker so out it would pour, and for as long as I was prepared to sit there and listen. On the few occasions when the flow did dry up, all it needed was a little prompt from me – 'And what happened then?' – and he would be off again: his travels, his plans for the future, his adventures with wild animals in the bush, the wonderful things he had seen and done in the big cities of Johannesburg and Cape Town and Durban. The tone was vain and conceited and although I recognised it as such, I was never really put off by it; if anything it only made his performance all the more riveting. But there was something else about those monologues that fascinated me almost as much as their content ... a strange, wild laugh that seemed to be their only form of punctuation.

I knew it wasn't *real* laughter. That much was obvious to me. I was already getting my first lessons in real laughter – in my opinion the most necessary of all the arts of survival – from a few very good teachers. In one secret little corner of my life – and for all I know that is where I might have gone after leaving Cousin Garth in his room – there was the joyous celebratory laughter of Sam and Willie, a sound I tried my best to capture in *Master Harold ... and the Boys*. In yet another there was my mother giving tongue to her broad vein of earthy, Afrikaner humour. Even then, at the age of ten, one or two of her 'jokes' made me squirm with embarrassment. I now realise that I have inherited that vein of vulgarity to the full and a few trusted friends know just how coarse it can be in my case. And let me not forget my dad. With his sly and slightly sardonic chuckles he was also teaching me a few appropriate responses to life's absurdities. I have been truly blessed in this regard – I really do think of it as one of my life's major blessings – and can look back now on a long line of wonderful teachers. And I am still learning. There is only one regret on this score, and that is that I have not been able to harness my love of laughter to the writing of a full-blooded comedy. I know that I have written a lot of very funny moments, and two plays in particular – *Hello and Goodbye* and *People Are Living There* – are at times fairly sustained exercises in laughter, but I still regret not having been

66

able to go the full distance. At one point I had a quote from Charlie Chaplin on the title page of *People Are Living There*:

If the flesh does not laugh in mockery and delight at the world
and at itself, then it will die.

The flesh! What a profound insight into the true nature of laughter to root it in our carnality, because surely that is what it really is, the most defiant of all the sounds of our mortality.

The sound that Garth made however had nothing to do with all of that. So what was it? If it wasn't true laughter, what was that strange noise that came out of him as effortlessly as the blinking of his ice-blue eyes? What was it in fact about Cousin Garth that had all of us, in varying degrees, responding to him with complicated strategies of avoidance? Because the more I watched and listened, the more I realised that there was something other than his drinking, or his often overwhelming body odours, or the fact that he couldn't keep a job, to explain the uneasiness we all felt in his presence. Then one afternoon there was a little incident which gave these vague, ill-defined feelings and questions a very specific reality on which my young mind could finally focus. My memory of the incident is so vivid I always play it back in the present tense.

My brother Royal and I are sprawled out on the floor of one of the Jubilee rooms, school books lying all around us. We are doing our homework. Mine consists of a map of the Union of South Africa showing the principal agricultural and industrial products of the various regions: gold in the Transvaal, maize in the Orange Free State, sugar in Natal and wine in the Cape. I can't remember what Royal was doing. Being older than me he was in a different class at school. Cousin Garth is sitting on a chair watching us. I am very proud of my map, the outline is clean and neat and for once without any smudges; the four provinces and protectorates have each been filled in with a different colour and my printing of the names of the major cities – Durban, Cape Town, Bloemfontein, Johannesburg and Port Elizabeth – looks very official. I get up from the floor and take it over to show it to Cousin Garth. I know I will be praised. I am his favourite. Sure enough the praise – in a voice smelling strongly of brandy – is lavish. And then it starts: 'And what about you Royal?' he asks. My brother looks up from the floor and I tense. There is a knot in the relationship between the two of them that I don't understand. There is also a sound in Garth's voice which I don't like. 'Come here,' Cousin Garth orders. Royal gets up and stands beside me in front of our cousin. 'Why don't you take a lesson from your younger brother?' he asks. Royal doesn't answer. He doesn't know what is going on. Neither do I. And then Garth does it. He leans forward and gives my brother a vicious, stinging slap full in the face …

And that is where the tape of memory runs out. I'm sure my brother cried, but I just can't remember. He certainly had every right to do so. I'm also fairly certain that I felt for him. What Cousin Garth had done was monstrously cruel and totally unjustified and I recognised it as such. But again I can't remember trying in any way to console or sympathise with Royal or to remonstrate with Garth. Whatever feelings I had at that moment were overshadowed by a sudden insight into the behaviour of my cousin: *With him things were never what they appeared to be.* All the other people in my life were acting and reacting in ways which by and large made a kind of sense even if I didn't always fully understand them. When for example, one Sunday night my mother picked up Royal and myself outside St Cuthberts Church where we were supposed to be singing in the choir, and then on the drive back home suddenly pulled the car over to the side of the road, turned around in the front seat and with demonic Greek fury beat the living daylights out of the two of us (with her heavy handbag) because she'd discovered (thanks to the snob Fugards) that Royal and I were playing truant, I lived through those bruising minutes in the car without any sense of injustice. We both knew that what we had done was wrong and that we deserved what we were getting. Or to take another example: the devious and sometimes dishonest manoeuvres my mother was forced to resort to, like the letters to landlords and creditors she made me write (her English wasn't good enough) with false excuses for being in arrears with rent and other payments … I knew what they were about, I was privy to her unending struggle to keep the family clothed and fed. There was a rationale to all of that which I had no difficulty in grasping.

Not so with Cousin Garth and that brutal slap to Royal's face. I knew

68

that his: 'Why don't you take a lesson from your brother?' was a lie, just a shabby cover-up for something else, and that that something else was well hidden away and most probably responsible for all of the dark aberrations in his behaviour. It was my first encounter with that complicated and tortuous pattern in human behaviour where men and women will act out a denial of themselves and their true natures because of inner pain and confusion. What I had discovered was that Cousin Garth had a secret, and it wasn't too long before I found out what it was.

❏   ❏   ❏

I have no memory at all of how it happened that Garth and I ended up one night sitting side by side on a bench on the Donkin. It was something we had never done before, and as far as I can remember it never happened again; there was just that once and I have tried time and time again to recall what led up to it, but without success. Like the narrow beam of a very powerful torch, my memory of what I believe was one of the seminal moments in my life as a writer has nothing else in its focus: just the two of us sitting there, Garth talking and me listening. There is no spread in either space or time. There are of course enough clues to fill in the blank canvas and build up a reasonably plausible picture around that central image and the circumstances which might have led up to it. To start with, it must have been a reasonably warm evening for the two of us to be up there in the first place. Most probably late summer or early autumn. Spring and early summer are the months when PE's famous winds blow. The Donkin is very exposed, and any hint of bad weather is quickly felt up there. And then the fact that it is dark … was it a casual walk after supper that had led my cousin by chance to where I was playing up there? … Sunday supper in all likelihood, because with all the Main Street bars closed there was nothing else for him to do. Or was there something more purposeful about it all? Needing somebody to talk to, had he deliberately sought me out and suggested the walk? And then a few details which memory would have recorded regardless of the time of year or the day of the week: the lighthouse sweeping its powerful beam across Algoa Bay every few seconds, with the smaller lights of Main Street at our feet and the more distant lights of ships at anchor out in the bay, waiting for the next day's berthing in the harbour. And while I'm about it let me fill in the sounds as well: the Town Hall clock chiming the hour and its quarters, the violent coupling of shunting trains down below in the railway yards, footfalls and indistinct murmurs of conversation as people passed on the paths that criss-crossed the Donkin, and somewhere near us, surely that most beautiful of all the evocations of the warm summer nights of my youth ... the chirping of a solitary cricket.

But all of that, however rich those specific details might be, is finally only conjecture. All I can tell you with absolute certainty when I try to remember that moment is that my hands are tucked in under my thighs – I am obviously wearing short trousers – and that both of them are clenched tightly on one of the horizontal wooden slats of the bench. The memory of my warm flesh and the feel of coarse grained wood polished smooth by hundreds of bums is very clear. I am tense and expectant, head lowered as I listen to Garth's voice. The conversation appears at first to be meandering casually along and about nothing in particular, but I am not fooled. There is something else involved. I am aware of a feeling coming from my cousin that I haven't encountered before – as if he is reaching out to me, and I don't know how to handle it. It is there particularly in his voice, which for the first time is without the vain show-off bluster and know-it-all tone with which he normally parades himself in public, and which I know so well and have come to despise. It is a voice which *makes* me listen to what he says. Although its tone is quiet and simple it nevertheless demands and commands my attention. The sound of it has lived with me as powerfully as his hysterical laugh, and has provided me with an infallible touchstone for the moment of truth in all my play writing.

In *Playland* the stage direction that leads into Gideon's confession is 'A voice shorn of all deception'. In *My Children! My Africa!* the equivalent stage direction for Mr M's moment is 'He makes his confession simply and truthfully'. In this vein I could work back through every play I have written and find in it a resonance, an echo of Garth's voice that night up there on the Donkin. The indelible memory of its naked and vulnerable quality as he opened himself to me has guided me as a director in

70

rehearsal rooms whenever I have tried to help actors embrace their own personal moment of truth. It is the voice with which we speak from the heart, the voice with which we lower all our defences and try to tell our deepest and most painful truths. Because that is what Garth was trying to do, and for all I know it might well have been the first time he had tried to do so. With one clumsy, halting sentence after another he finally blundered into this confession:

'I'm not like other men … I'm not interested in girls … I'm different … I like to be with men and boys … Some people are born that way … I am one of them …'

And then finally, when he had got it all out:

'You understand don't you, Hally?' I remember nodding, and whispering a barely audible 'Yes'.

It was a hugely complex moment for me. His confession left me struggling with powerful and contradictory emotions. My first instinctive response had been one of fear, that it was the prelude to him asking for or trying to do something I couldn't handle. I wanted to jump up and run back to the safety of the Jubilee and my family. But at the same time there was something about the moment and the sound of his voice which made my believe I could trust him. As it turned out, in all the time we sat up there on the bench talking, he never once made even the smallest attempt to touch me. As for understanding him? That was the biggest surprise of all: I did. If there was any shock at all in the experience it was in discovering that I *already knew* his secret. From almost the first few words of his confession, something in me had jumped ahead and had known what was coming: somehow I had tapped into a fund of secret knowledge inside myself that I never knew I had. It was my first experience of that most essential of all the writers' faculties – intuition. But as surprising as was its discovery, even more so were the emotions it provoked: a surge of dark elation, a thrilling sense of power.

❏ ❏ ❏

I only properly understood and appreciated what was involved in that moment with Garth years later and it happened in the most round about way. If I remember correctly, it was Barney Simon, writer, director, Artistic Director of the Market Theatre and a close friend of forty years standing, who introduced me to Edward S Curtis's photographs of the North American Indians. I am indebted to him in similar fashion for many other treasures in my life. What I am very certain about, however, because it still happens every time I look at it, is the thrill of recognition I experienced as I paged through that first book.

To start with, the instant, electrifying appeal of the spiritual austerity so magnificently captured in his portraits. They were such a powerful contrast and antidote to the corrosive materialism of my own culture. Through them I caught a glimpse of a way of life that flowed effortlessly out of a harmony with and reverence for nature rather than the exploitation of it that so disastrously characterises our civilisation. From the moment I saw them I felt a very ancient affinity with those faces.

I have two major physical needs when it comes to my writing habits: total privacy and immediate access to nature. The latter is as simple and direct as being able to stand up at my desk, take a few steps, and be under a tree – which is possible in both my Port Elizabeth and Karoo homes where I do all my writing. I have tried several times and without any success whatsoever, to write in flats and apartments in cities. It's a waste of time, nothing comes. In the course of this morning's session for example – I've been working on this section in Port Elizabeth – I've been around my very unruly garden at least half a dozen times already, and these excursions were in no sense interruptions to my work – I went on composing and editing in my head as effectively as if I had stayed at my desk. If anything, a well-timed exit into the garden to look at a flower, or a tree, or a bird, gives the battery a boost rather than draining it. But I mustn't make it sound trite. A very complicated process is at work here, involving, among other things, daily instruction in humility, natural reverence and patience. Impoverished as my contacts with nature are when compared to the profound communion those Indians had, they nevertheless do give me a sense of remote kinship.

But over the years I kept being nagged by a vague sense that there was something else I needed to understand about those faces and the lifestyle so tantalisingly glimpsed in those photographs. I eventually found it in Frithjof Schuon's introduction to *Light on The Ancient Worlds*, the fifth book of prints I acquired.

A fascinating combination of combative and stoical heroism with a priestly bearing conferred on the Indian of the Plains and Forests a sort of majesty at once aquiline and solar; hence the powerful original and irreplaceable beauty that is associated with the red man and contributes to his prestige as a warrior and a martyr. Like the Japanese of the time of the Samurai, the Red Indian was in the deepest sense an artist in the outward manifestations of his personality: apart from the fact that his life was a ceaseless sporting with suffering and death, hence also a kind of chivalrous Karma yoga, the Indian knew how to impart to his spiritual style an aesthetic adornment unsurpassable in its expressiveness.

'One factor which may have caused people to regard the Red Indian as an individualist – in principle and not merely de facto – is the crucial importance he attaches to moral worth in men – to character if you will – and hence his cult of action. The whole Red Indian character may be summed up in two words, if such a condensation be allowable: *the act and the secret: the act shattering if need be, and the secret impassive.* Rock-like, the Indian of former times rested in his own being, his own personality, ready to translate it into action with the impetuosity of lightning; but at the same time he remained humble before the Great Mystery, whose message he knew, could always be discerned in the Nature around him.

[The italics are mine.]

❏   ❏   ❏

I cannot imagine a simpler and, at the same time more insightful penetration of the nature of creativity than the coupling of those two words: secret and action. That polarity perfectly describes what I believe is the essential dynamic of my writing. When I read those words I properly understand for the first time the dark elation, the sense of power I had experienced through Garth's confession on the Donkin bench. In opening his heart to me Garth had given me my first empowerment as a writer. Because that is my real territory as a dramatist: the world of secrets, with their powerful effect on human behaviour and the trauma of their revelation. Whether it is the radiant secret in Miss Helen's heart or the withering one in Boesman's or the dark and destructive one in Gladys, they are the dynamos that generate all the significant action in my plays.

My first and last word of advice to any young writer remains: guard your secrets jealously.

To return briefly to that moment with Garth on the Donkin, our exit from it is as obscured by the fog of time and bad memory as was our entrance. Did it end with a silent walk back to the Jubilee … together? Did I lie in bed that night before sleep, thinking about what Garth had revealed to me? And when I woke up the next day, what effect, if any, did it have on our relationship? The answer to all those questions is, yet again, I don't remember. Shortly afterwards my cousin did another one of his disappearing tricks. Our next meeting would be five years later, and in a very different world.

❏   ❏   ❏

And so, finally, suburbia, and what was to be the last of the family homes: 73 Third Avenue, Newton Park. It was a prototype middle-class white South African world: square, solid brick houses with small manicured gardens in front, a servant's room in the back yard and a notice: Beware of the Dog – Lumkele Inja – on just about every gate. And of course walls. High walls, low walls, ornamental walls, wire-mesh and split-pole fencing … it made no difference what you used, just as long as your piece of God's earth was safely behind walls … an appropriate metaphor for the wary, and guarded adolescence I carried into the house on the corner of Hudson Street and Third Avenue. I was fifteen years old and a Standard Seven pupil at the Port Elizabeth Technical College.

My high school education was well on its way to being an unmitigated disaster. A Standard Six essay on butterfly hunting in the Amazon River basin – I was already a very keen amateur naturalist – had

74

been rewarded with a four year scholarship in motor mechanics at the PE 'Tech'. Apart from the two official languages, English and Afrikaans, there was nothing in the curriculum of those four years of high schooling that fostered and encouraged my real interests in any way, or helped me locate myself in the world. All my energies were being directed, with a singular lack of success, to lathes and milling machines, electrical circuitry and the mysteries of the internal combustion engine. I even spent one term at a blacksmith's forge trying to hammer out horseshoes. The futility and waste of all that effort was neatly summed up one day in my final year by a little moment in the class in technical drafting, which was one of my subjects. We were all at work on a typical assignment: drafting the three projections of a clutch plate, or a cylinder head, or something else that made rattles under a motorcar bonnet. All around me the earnest young engineers of the future were bent in deep concentration over their drawing boards, hard at work with needle sharp 4H pencils, T-squares and precision drawing instruments. The latter were kept and cherished in little purple velvet-lined cases as lovingly as I now keep my fountain pens and pencils in a soft leather jewellery roll. Pacing quietly up and down the rows – there were about twenty of us – and pausing from time to time to help a pupil with a word of advice or encouragement was our instructor, 'Big Bill' Hamilton. He would occasionally even take up a pencil or a compass to show them a trick or two. He was an impressive man, over six feet tall, with the rugged good looks of a Robert Ryan or a Gary Cooper. Even though his 'six of the best' were acknowledged by us pupils as being more painful than those of any of the other teachers, I detected a great deal of sensitivity in him and really liked him. I was absolutely useless at drafting, and on this particular day I think it was more obvious than usual. When Mr Hamilton stopped at my desk and looked down at the grubby mess of smudges and erasures defacing the square yard of once immaculately white drawing paper, he audibly sounded the wave of defeat and helplessness that overwhelmed him. When the groan had died away, he just stood there looking at my mess and shaking his head and murmuring 'Fugard… Fugard… Fugard…' He was at a loss for words. I was so obviously beyond being helped and guided with those quiet little suggestions he would whisper to the other boys when he stood next to them. We stood there in silence for a few moments as I waited with a matching sense of helplessness. It was in fact a small moment of genuine comradeship between the two of us, because looking down at my work I knew exactly what he was feeling. There just was no hope for the author of those smudges.

On my desk next to the drafting board was the stack of library books that had by then become a permanent part of the baggage I carried around with me wherever I went. Mr Hamilton turned his attention from the drafting board to the titles of the books. At that point in my reading it would have been a mixed bag – some nature and African adventure, Alexander Dumas maybe, and possibly even a Tolstoy or a Faulkner. 'You like reading,' he observed. I said yes. Another pause and then, after a few awkward hesitations he came straight to the point. 'Fugard... why don't you think about becoming a librarian when you leave school. You know, something connected with books. Wouldn't you like that?' 'Yes I would,' I said. There was another painful silence while we turned our attention back to the mess on the drawing board. 'You don't enjoy doing that do you?' he asked, pointing at my attempt at a clutch plate or whatever it was. 'No I don't,' I said emphatically. It was such a huge relief to be able to tell the truth that I repeated myself ... 'I really don't.' He nodded his approval of my honesty. 'So talk to your folks about it ... a librarian or something like that. One of the most important things in life, Fugard, is to be happy in your work' ... and with those very wise words, he resumed his patrolling of the desks.

If the time and circumstances had been right for a proper chat with Mr Hamilton I would in fact have told him that at that point I didn't yet know what I wanted to do with my life – a healthy uncertainty that was to continue right into my third year at university. As I saw it, there were three powerful and warring options open to me – literature, music and science ... particularly the biological sciences. By the time I sat down in 'Doc' Bromley's Standard Seven English class in my first year at the Tech, I was already a confirmed word addict. The three page, five hundred-word school compositions which the other boys struggled to complete were usually about twenty pages and several thousand words long by the time I had finished with the subject. That stack of library books I was carrying around with me was, of course, another clue as to what the future was finally going to be about, to say nothing of those sessions with Johnnie which I have already described. But at the time I am writing about, my desire to be able to sit down at the piano and make music for myself was every bit as powerful as my *scribendi cacoethes* (incurable itch to write). To this day I still fantasise about being at the piano and sweeping away audiences, and myself, with playing of stunning virtuosity. I've never had a single fantasy about the writing of or performance of one of my plays.

From the age of eight through to my last year at the Tech, a series of piano teachers – classical and jazz – tried hard but unsuccessfully to turn me into an accomplished pianist. The operative word is 'accomplished'. It was easy enough for me to sit down and give a fair but stilted reading of the piece of sheet music open in front of me – Liszt's 'Lieberstraum' or Jerome Kern's 'Look for the Silver Lining'. But there was no way that I was going to settle for a 'fair reading'. What I wanted was that extraordinary magical freedom that Johnnie's hands had when he sat down at the piano, a freedom not only to render what was on the printed page, but to play and improvise with it, to slip effortlessly out of one tune and into another, and even to make music that had never before seen a printed page. What I didn't realise or appreciate at the time is that my hands, my right hand to be precise, already had something of that freedom when it put pencil to blank paper and played with words. But I never mastered it at the keyboard. Apart from a lack of innate musicality there was another factor that put paid to my musical ambitions: my hands were too small and just not capable of the stretch that classical music demands. The moment when those ambitions crashed discordantly came one afternoon in the middle of an attempt to master a particularly difficult Chopin prelude. I was having a lot of trouble trying to get the fingering right. I broke off my playing abruptly and lowered my hands into my lap. I savoured the heavy silence in the room for a few seconds then said aloud: 'Give it up chum, you're wasting your time'. I carefully replaced the green felt dust cover over the keys, lowered the keyboard cover and never opened it again.

The most serious contender of all my options at that time, though, was unquestionably science. It was an authentic passion, on a par with literature and music, and although it is now only vestigially present in my life I am convinced that a few serendipitous accidents at the time might well have made it the winner and given my story a very different ending. Proof of my passion is the fact that I was completely self-taught in my considerable knowledge of biology until my final year at the Tech when I discovered its Pharmacy School and was able to attend night classes there in chemistry and biology. Microbiology in particular fired my imagination. To this day I still believe that a drop of pond water under a microscope with reasonable magnification is the best free adventure show on earth. I spent many breathless hours watching the titanic battles between the denizens of that brief little universe. Many years later I couldn't wait for my daughter Lisa to be old enough so that I could use her as an excuse to justify buying a microscope for me to play with. I still do from time to time. It occurred to me the other day that this is really just another, but acceptable form of the 'peeping through the keyhole' syndrome that I indulged in during the Jubilee years. It certainly engenders the same breathless thrill. It all comes back to secrets, doesn't it?

When we moved into the Newton Park house I immediately commandeered the empty servant's room in the back yard and set it up as my laboratory, with my microscope, chemistry set and, most ominously of all, my dissecting kit. A series of terrible 'mad scientist' experiments on frogs and a few other poor creatures still haunt my Buddhist conscience. I remember very clearly the awe with which I looked down at the beating heart of the first frog – anaesthetised with a swab of chloroform – that I opened up. I even dragged poor Sam at the St George's Park Tea Room into it by leaving him in charge of the post-operative care of my 'patients' – with very specific instructions about catching and feeding flies to them – while I trudged off reluctantly to the workshops of the PE Tech. Many were the bitter and accusatory harangues I inflicted on him when I returned later to find the patient dead at the bottom of the intensive care jam jar.

My interest in science was coupled with one in philosophy. I spent as much time pondering the ultimate riddles of the universe as I did pumping Gentian Violet into the arterial system of a *Platana*. In fact the literary exercise I remember most clearly from these years is not a poem, or short story, or the start of a novel, but a statement of the first principles of a brand new philosophic system based on Darwinian evolution, which I firmly believed would finally put all religions out of business – I was at the time a virulent little atheist. It was one hundred and fifty foolscap pages long, and was hand written during one of the long school holidays when I was earning pocket money as a locker room attendant at the St George's Park Swimming Bath. It was my passion for science and philosophy that led to my escape from a possible career as the world's worst motor mechanic and landed me on the campus of the University of Cape Town. Literature and music had nothing to do with the subjects I selected for my degree: social science, social anthropology, ethics and metaphysics, and political philosophy. It was only degree re-quirements that forced me very reluctantly to include a year of French in my studies, and it was the one subject that gave me no joy whatsoever. Fortunately for me, through my friendship with the poet Perseus Adams, writing stayed open as an option in my life. When we first met on the UCT campus Perseus was studying psychology, but there was no doubt in his mind that poetry was his destiny, and time was to prove him right. We were both campus misfits and spent all our free time together either railing against the 'bourgeois' (quite definitely our favourite word) or in long, rambling and exhausting conversations about the books and poems we loved. My escape from the world of science and philosophy and the trap of an academic career came when, just prior to the final exams for my degree, the two of us decided to embrace our identity as writers, and hitch-hike up from Cape Town to Cairo. In a wonderful closing of ranks by the arts against the sciences, it was that already mentioned session with Beethoven's Seventh Symphony at the College of Music library that gave me the courage to take the leap. In a letter to my mother I tried my best to explain the identity crisis I had just worked my way through, and my sense that I was meant to be a writer and that the first class univer-sity degree I was on the point of getting and for which she had slogged and slaved and scrimped and saved was a trap. I posted the letter and

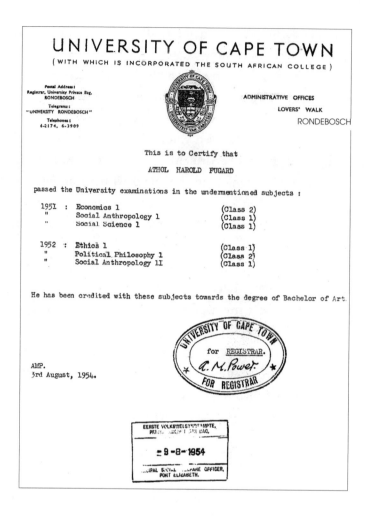

held my breath. Her letter back of support and faith in me was a blessing, surpassed only by the very first one she gave me in bringing me into this world. But that pivotal moment was still a good few years ahead of me as I drudged my way through the four years of the motor mechanics course at the Technical College.

The Newton Park house wasn't truly a 'family home' in the sense of a place where we all came together to tie and untie that rosary of knots that is every family's unique story. In our case that happened in the St George's Park Tea Room; very little family life was lived out in 73 Third Avenue. I honestly can't remember a single family gathering or even a family meal in it during those years. My strongest memory of the house itself is the heavy suburban silence that always suffocated the music that

The author with his parents in the Newton Park house where
'very little family life was lived out'

I tried to make at the piano in the lounge – the old Fritz Kuhla had travelled with us from the Jubilee and was once again the centrepiece of a dead and joyless room.

There were four bedrooms in the house, and it was in them that you found signs of life. My parents' room in the front was the largest, and eventually became an important inspiration and model for my play *Hello and Goodbye*. My mother was a compulsive hoarder, and all the rubbish that she hadn't been able to throw away when we packed up and left the Jubilee, and again when we packed up and left the Cape Road smallholding, and again when she finally packed up and left the St George's Park Tea Room, all of that rubbish – it is itemised in the play –

ended up in cardboard boxes and suitcases and bags and biscuit tins under beds and on top of already jam packed wardrobes and chests of drawers. It was a nightmare, and I think partly explains the great and abiding pleasure I always experience when I move into an impersonal and empty hotel room. I am now as manic about throwing away my rubbish as my mother was in hoarding hers. The other bedrooms were my sister's – appropriately feminine and chintzy, a spare bedroom which at various times was occupied by a succession of quite interesting paying boarders, and then finally, the bedroom I shared with my brother. With its windows facing the west it was the warmest room in the house and free of the sunless chill in which the others were permanently locked. I can still feel the warmth of the afternoon flood of golden sunlight that used to pour into it. But most important of all, it became my first private space, because shortly after we moved into the house my brother left Port Elizabeth to pursue his career as a horticulturist in Durban.

It was in this room that my dad and I settled down every Sunday afternoon during my last year at the Tech to listen to the BBC series on the lives and music of Gilbert and Sullivan. It was in this room that I eventually packed my haversack for my hitch-hike down to Cape Town and the start of my three years at university. As that moment approached, my excitement at the prospect of freedom and the intellectual adventure that lay ahead was overshadowed by the pain and guilt of leaving my dad. There had always been a special bond between us, and now with the departure of my brother for Durban and my sister for boarding school, and with my mother busy at the tea room from early morning until late at night, we had grown even closer, and his dependence on me had increased. Marooned as he was in the house by deteriorating health, my departure meant that he was going to be a very lonely man – a prospect that frightened him and savaged me with guilt.

On my last afternoon in the room he hobbled in on his crutches, in his hands, still in its factory wrapping, the shirt *I* had given *him* as a Christmas present a few months earlier. This time around it was a parting present from him to me, and he handed it over tearfully. It was awful – his sobbing misery, my tears and sense of betrayal and desertion – another pivotal image in *Hello and Goodbye* that I owe to that house.

Father and son outside the Newton Park house – 'There had always been a special bond between us'

But unlike the Johnny of my play, I did not look back and relent. Early the next morning, after coffee and bread and jam with my mother, I strode out into the Cape road and started to thumb passing cars.

Two years later, when I had hitch-hiked back home during a university break, it was in this room late at night that the sight of my brother, who was also home for a short holiday and was fast asleep in bed, gave me the seminal image and experience for *The Bloodknot* – the watershed play I was to write ten years later. And finally, it is in this room that I find myself in the last of my boyhood memories of Garth. No dark epiphanies this time. The appropriate adjectives are 'sad' and 'predictable'.

❏ ❏ ❏

His, as usual unannounced, appearance was in every respect a repeat performance of the many in the past, the only difference on this occasion being the setting. It was in the tea room that I discovered him when I trudged in disconsolately after another wasted day in the workshops of

83

the PE Tech. He was sitting at a table with my mother, between them the remains of a pot of tea and a silence with more frosting on it than the stale doughnuts on the counter. When he saw me he sprang to his feet and with his usual bluster opened his arms for a warm-hearted embrace which I evaded – physical contact with him had always been an off-putting prospect. Under some very shallow pretext, which I am perfectly certain did not fool Garth, my mother and I retired to the kitchen for the furiously whispered exchange that was one of the many modes of communication between the two of us. A viciously repeated 'Get rid of him!' was all I had to say. I was going through a difficult time, both at school and at home, and the last thing I wanted in my life was my boozing cousin with all his complications and nonsense. My mother on the other hand was inclined to be more generous: he was family and he needed a place to sleep and food to eat. Eventually, and with very bad grace, I agreed to let him move into my room and Royal's bed – 'But only for a few days understand, otherwise…' and then a look that was meant to indicate the most dire consequences if my wishes were ignored – we Fugards were all masters of emotional blackmail.

The simple truth of the matter is that my relationship with Garth had outgrown its earlier innocence. On his side, apart from his boozer's flush being a shade deeper and that laugh a decibel more hysterical, it appeared to be the same old Garth as far as I could see. But on mine it was most definitely not the same young Hally. The first time he called me that, I icily corrected him and told him that my name was now Athol Fugard. With adolescence I had become very introverted, in addition to which my cousin no longer fascinated me in the way that he had. Now he was just another 'homo' and that was the end of it. I knew all about Oscar Wilde and *De Profundis* and had also read *The Well of Loneliness*.

However, once I had got over my initial resentment at his intrusion, the situation in my room settled down and became tolerable enough. During the day he was out trying to find a job – as usual that had been one of his first promises – while I was busy at the Tech cramming for my final Matriculation exams. It was only at night that we saw each other and then he would either join me in listening quietly to the classical

84

Mother, father and Willie outside the St George's Park Tea Room

musical concerts and recitals on the wireless – he had a genuine love of good music – or lose himself in one of my library books if I was busy with homework. Neither of us made any mention of, or in any way acknowledged that moment on the Donkin bench.

It is possible I suppose that if left like this we might have gone on to rediscover each other and build a new relationship. There was certainly enough substance for that possibility. Apart from the family bond both of us were lonely – me in my confused adolescence and he in his homosexuality – and true companionship was a very real need in both of our lives. It would indeed have been a very rich one because of our shared appreciation of music and good literature, in addition to which I was going to discover many many years later that Garth was also harbouring literary ambitions. But our story was to have a different ending.

If I had been writing a play the stage directions for the last scene between us would look something like this:

[*The bedroom, early evening. A more than usually flushed and sweating Garth, still in his clothes, is sprawled out on a bed. The wireless, with its volume turned up unnecessarily loud, is blaring out pop music and Garth, in spite of not knowing the words, is trying to sing along. The bedroom door opens suddenly and Athol steps into the room. Garth sits upright on the bed and with an inane grin and open arms welcomes his cousin. Athol does not respond. He stands very still, staring back fixedly at Garth.*]

It was the smell of brandy that did it. With a sinking feeling I knew what I was in for, and sure enough the moment he saw me he turned off the radio and launched into one of his rambling monologues. Nothing would stop him – not the wireless when I turned it on again and very loud, not my homework, not even a lunatic half hour of scales and arpeggios on the old Fritz Kuhla in the lounge when I sat down at the piano in an attempt to escape his madness. He simply followed me into the room, collapsed on a sofa, and carried on talking while I charged up and down the keyboard like a demented young Liszt. There was nothing left finally but to use darkness to bring down the curtain on the crazy little scene we were acting out. With what I hoped was a voice of authority that brooked no argument, I announced: 'Bed time. Let's go to sleep Garth.' I switched off the light in the middle of one of his interminable sentences, undressed in the dark, and got into bed. It actually seemed to work; he stopped talking, and, as I lay there drifting off to sleep all I could hear was his heavy breathing. The next thing I knew was that someone was lifting the sheets and crawling into bed beside me. I was wide awake in an instant. The rancid smell of brandy and body odours was overpowering. I pushed away the hand that had settled on my thigh and spoke quietly, but firmly. 'No Garth. Get out.' A breathless pause. The other body didn't move. 'Get out Garth!' Another few seconds of tense silence, and then he got out as wordlessly as he had got in. I lay awake for a long time, rigid with tension, waiting for him to try again, but nothing happened. In the morning when I woke up Garth was gone and on the kitchen table was a short note thanking my mom and dad for their hospitality. Thirty-five years would pass before I saw him again.

❑ ❑ ❑

At another level Garth remained very much an 'absent presence' in my life. That moment on the Donkin when he had bared his soul spun itself out into a thread which was to run through all those intervening years until we met again, for the last time. In my first year at university my one meaningful friendship – Perseus Adams came in my second year – was with a fellow student several years older than me who was gay. Johan was a trained nurse and was studying for a diploma in social work. Although he believed I was also gay our relationship remained nothing more than a friendship because he already had a partner in his life, a German businessman with whom he lived. I think however that it was the aura of this friendship that led me into my brief and one and only sexual relationship with another man. He was much older than I was and I met him when Johan and I were hitch-hiking around the country. He had stopped and given us a lift in Zululand. I did not find the relationship fulfilling however, and after a few months I broke it off. There has been no inclination since then to repeat the experience.

From time to time, however I continue to encounter 'suspicions' that I am in fact gay. The most recent was only a year or so ago when I was in New Bethesda by myself, writing *Playland*. There was a knock on my front door one afternoon and I opened it to find two young women on my doorstep. They had impulsively driven up to the village from Cape Town after seeing Yvonne Bryceland's radiant performance in the film of *The Road to Mecca*. Somebody had mentioned to them that I was in the village, and they had come around to say hello. I joined them for a stroll along the quiet tree-lined streets and a richly rewarding conversation about Helen Martins, her life and her work, and what a powerful role model she was for all young South African women – white and black – in this male chauvinistic society. As we were parting, one of them, a professional ballet dancer, suddenly asked 'Are you gay?' Because the question was so unexpected I was taken aback for a few seconds and then answered, 'No'. We parted. Later that night there was another knock on the door. It was the dancer, and this time she was alone. She was visibly distressed, and wasted no time in blurting out that she was deeply mortified and ashamed of herself for intruding on my privacy by asking if I was gay ... she had no right to pry ... she was deeply ashamed and asked my forgiveness ... what I did with my life was nobody's business ... she wouldn't let me say a word until she had literally run out of breath. Then she listened quietly while I thanked her for her concern and assured her that no harm had been done. We parted friends. I hope I meet her again.

What it all comes down to finally I suppose is the sort of relationship you have with the opposite sexual aspect of your nature which is there inside all of us. I would like to believe that I have a very easy and open one with mine. I know I have direct access to it when I write. I have been asked many times how, as a man, I have managed to be as intimate with the female psyche as the portraits of the women in my plays have revealed. Or in a different area, the parallel but much more angry question: 'How could you as a white presume to write about the black experience?' The answer to both is the same: there is one truly winged aspect of our natures which allows us to escape the confines and limits of our own personal experience and penetrate others that we have never had ... the human imagination. My own personal interpretation of the Prometheus legend is that that is the real fire he stole for us from the gods.

4

EPILOGUE

It was a cold, wet, lonely, and in every other possible way misery sodden Cape Town winter. My play, *A Place with the Pigs* in which I was acting together with the wonderful Lida Meiring, was fighting for its life at the Baxter Theatre. I had suffered the not uncommon fate of a writer who confounds the critics by exploring a new direction – their reviews had been savage. With the intellectual laziness that characterises so many of them, they had sat there half asleep, waiting for me to repeat tried and tested formulas of the past, and of course had been disappointed. By the time they woke up and realised that something different was happening on stage it was too late – the play was over. Cape Town audiences are also no different from those in most other large cities in being quite happy to have the critics do their thinking for them. The end result of all this is that Lida and I were playing to only a handful of people every night.

Looking back now over the thirty-five years that I have been writing I can see something in the way of a ten year cycle to my work, each turn of the wheel being marked by the writing of an aberrant play. There have been three of these 'aberrations' to date: *Orestes, Dimetos* and most recently, *Pigs*. Writing each of them was an exceptionally hard and painful process accompanied by huge emotional disturbance – so much so that I think of these three plays as my 'literary breakdowns'. The reason for their overload of trauma and angst is the fact that they all marked the start of a regenerative process and that, by its very nature, is bound to be painful. This also happens to be the central theme of *Pigs*, which made the experience doubly harrowing – having first had to write the damned thing, I was now up there on stage six nights a week acting it out! The hell of it all was given a further boost, not that it needed it, by the fact that this was only my second play since I'd stopped drinking. The first one was *The Road to Mecca*, and as had been the case with that, I was again floundering helplessly in a quagmire of self-doubt and panic. That little voice inside me was very insistent, telling me all the time that my creativity needed a certain percentage of alcohol in my bloodstream in order to function. During the writing of *Pigs* on The Ashram, my home on the outskirts of Port Elizabeth, these fears and doubts used to make me physically ill at my desk. My only escape from them, and it never lasted very long, was to drive madly down to Sardinia Bay and then try to run away from myself as fast as I could on the beach. The terrors were still with me in Cape Town, and this time they had me pounding furiously up and down the Sea Point beach front. The wilder the weather – and a few really major South Atlantic gales blew in during this period – the easier it was for me to face up to the long stretch that still lay ahead of me … the Johannesburg run at the Market Theatre and what I anticipated would be an equally negative response from the critics up there. On the latter score I was wrong – the play was very favourably reviewed.

If my circumstances in Cape Town had been different, with the play a huge success and my days filled with all the congratulatory noise and excitement that goes with a 'hit', if I had been leaving the theatre each night flushed with pride and satisfaction instead of slipping out of it as if I had done something unmentionable on stage, would I have responded differently to the letter from Garth which I found waiting for me at the Baxter Theatre one night? Probably yes. A sad admission to make, but unfortunately it happens to be the truth – in all likelihood I would have ignored it. I'm fairly certain it was a combination of my loneliness and the guilt-ridden angst of both the play and my mental state at the time, that made me respond. There had been a few other letters from him to my mom and dad during the years since Newton Park, but they had all been greeted by a stony silence on our side. We remained steadfast in our prejudices and fear of the '…well-known Cape pederast' which is how one member of the family described him in hushed tones.

The handwritten letter in my dressing room at the Baxter was one page long:

Dear Cousin,

A croaky voice from your past! I don't mean to intrude on what I am sure is a very busy time for you but I just could not resist the temptation to drop you a line. I am living in digs not too far from the theatre and I was wondering if by any chance you wanted to meet up again after all these years. If you do, drop me a line or give a tinkle. I do however appreciate how busy you must be and if you don't find it possible I will of course understand. In the meantime, good luck with the show. My health is rather poorly at the moment so I don't know if I'll get a chance to see it.

Your ever loving cousin.

Garth.

I didn't respond immediately, my first reaction being that I was indeed 'too busy' doing nothing to make contact with him. There is a moment in *Dimetos* when Sophia says to my anti-hero: 'Yours is unquestionably the most selfish soul I have ever known.' The line came originally from the mouth of Yvonne Bryceland and she had directed it, with total justification, at me. True generosity of spirit is a virtue I admire and envy more than any other. I am particularly selfish about my time and energy, which I hoard like a wretched miser for my work. I resent and do everything I can to avoid any other demands on them. But I felt guilty about Garth and that put a brake on my first impulse to throw his letter into the trash can in my dressing room. We 'frightened Fugards' had nothing to be proud of in our relationship with the 'wicked' branch of the family, particularly during the last years of my Uncle Garth's life when word reached us that he and my Aunt Dulcie had fallen on hard times. It would have cost us so little to reach out to them, but we didn't. In addition to my guilty feelings on this score, a little instinct cautioned me to think twice before ignoring a hand extended in friendship. A few days after receiving the letter from Garth at the Baxter, I made the call, and at the end of a stilted and absurdly formal exchange on the telephone I arranged to visit him at his digs.

His directions led me to a back street in a part of Cape Town that had seen better days. At one time it had obviously been a comfortable middle-class white suburb like Newton Park. Now it was a run down and rather shabby 'grey area', a victim of the population pressures in the inner city, with white and coloured families living side by side, the latter no doubt hoping desperately that they had escaped the clutches of the infamous Group Areas Act. The house itself, behind a weed-choked postage stamp of neglected garden, had burglar bars on all the windows and a security gate on the front door. The only photograph I have of Garth from this period is a snapshot of him in the little garden standing in front of a nondescript and bedraggled shrub. There is, however, enough detail in it for me to recognise a Fugard behind the pasty, sagging features staring morosely at the camera. On the occasion of my visit, however, they were smiling self-consciously as he opened the front door and unlocked the security gate. After awkward and overly-effusive greetings on the little polished red stoep he stepped to one side and with a theatrical flourish invited me into the house. Security gate and front door were then locked and bolted again very carefully before he led me down a dark little passage to his room at the back. For a few seconds I could have believed myself back in our old Newton Park home: the hushed and musty silence that filled the house was the same as that which used to smother my piano playing, and as I followed Garth down the little passageway I experienced once again a wave of that dry suburban despair that would wash over me in that house on the corner of Hudson Street.

At the end of the passage another theatrical flourish ushered me into his room and then into a comfortable cane chair. He immediately started fussing with a tea tray which had obviously been laid out for my visit, giving me a chance to form first impressions. They were very favourable, my cousin had aged surprisingly well. Although his financial circumstances were desperate – a miserable pension barely covered rent and food, while the charity of a local Catholic church provided second-hand clothes and other personal needs – he was nevertheless clean shaven and neatly dressed and … yes, no question about it, it was the face of a Fugard. For all its aging and sagging sensualism there was still a hint of the silver-haired, patrician good looks my father had aged into. The room itself also reflected a sense of personal pride and dignity. Above his bed hung a crucifix, and on the opposite wall a palm-leaf cross and one of those dreadful lithographs of Christ pointing at his thorn-encircled heart – Garth had converted to Catholicism some years previously. A few books were lined up neatly on a little shelf on another wall while a bedside table had a Bible and ashtray.

Sitting there listening and watching, I had a nagging sense that we were re-enacting a little scene that had already been scripted and acted out somewhere else. Then it came to me in a flash: my very earliest memory of my cousin in that little back room of the Jubilee, as I sat on the bed and watched him while he unpacked his battered old suitcase. It was an uncanny sensation, as if that scene from the past had gone through a sort of time warp, leaving some of its elements intact while blurring and changing others. Instead of a glass of brandy in his hand, there was now a cup of tea – and one in mine as well! Instead of my short-trousered legs swinging in the air, they were now in faded denim jeans and planted firmly on the floor. But on the other hand completely unchanged was the effortless and uninterrupted flow of words as he talked about himself, and equally unchanged was my fascination as I listened to him. The laugh was also still there, irrationally punctuating his monologue, although its character had changed. It wasn't dangerous anymore. It had a hollow, slightly sepulchral ring to it now, and appropriately the one subject he kept returning to was his failing health and a very serious heart condition which should have made him 'food for the worms ages ago … (big laugh)'. With a flash of his old conceit he told me that the doctor in charge of his case was going to deliver a paper on him at the next congress of the South African Medical Association, there being aspects of his heart condition that made it unique in the annals of medical history.

His other main theme was the politics of the house and an ongoing feud with a Polish boarder in one of the front rooms. At stake were the small favours and affections of Mrs Gabriella da Souza, the landlady. By that I don't mean to suggest that Garth had changed his sexual preference. On the contrary, he made it perfectly clear to me by way of a few hints and heavy innuendo that nothing had changed in that directions except for the fact that his heart condition had now ruled out his having any 'real fun anymore'. It had forced him to give up drinking and smoking and a '… few other delights of the flesh, if you catch my drift cousin' … followed by a wink and a laugh. 'Favours and affections' simply meant having Gabriella's permission to plug in an electric heater when it got cold instead of having to hide it away in the wardrobe and only take it out late at night when she was unlikely to make a sudden appearance at the door, or being invited to join her on the sofa in the lounge for a couple of hours of TV at night. My arrival on the scene – his 'famous cousin' – had given him a sudden and huge advantage over the Polish interloper in the front room. There was nothing *he* could play that would trump the way the name Fugard was being splashed about in the papers. My ready consent to having afternoon tea with Mrs Da Souza had him gloating like a Rumplestiltskin who knew he finally had the pretty maiden in his clutches.

His life centred on the weekly visits of the ambulance that took him to Groote Schuur Hospital where his heart condition was being monitored, and the Catholic priest who came once a week to say Mass. The nearest Catholic church was too far for him to walk to. For the rest, he did his best to fill his spare time by listening to the radio – his appreciation of good music remained intact – and by reading. The one thing he regretted most about his bad health was that it had forced him to stop singing in the church choir. When he had told me this I had flashbacked yet again to an image from the past: Garth singing lustily in the Salvation Army circle at the bottom of Donkin Street. He also mentioned a Good Samaritan friend who kept an eye on him and helped out in various ways.

During the four weeks that were left of the play's run in Cape Town I visited Garth another three times. Two of them were to take him out to lunch, followed by a drive around the Peninsula, and the other was to take him up to the Baxter so that he could see my play. After the show we went back to his room and brewed up a late-night pot of Rooibos. We settled down with our mugs of tea and ambled into a relaxed and easy discussion of the play. I knew that Garth had had as much, if not a damned sight more, experience of being in pigsties as I had, and I had hoped that he would see what the play was really getting at. To my huge satisfaction he had, and at every level: the humour, the absurdity, the pathos, and most important of all, the possibility of personal redemption. Eventually:

'That scene where you wore the dress!'
'You liked it?'
'You bet. Bloody good laugh it was. But I've never wanted to try that one myself you know.'
'Never?'
'No. Not my style.'
'What have you tried?'
'Everything else!'

... and after a huge laugh he was off and it once again became a question of just sitting back in the cane chair and letting the flow of his words carry me along. This time, however, it was the quintessential Garth. The play had made a deep impression on him, and he was quietly thoughtful in a way I had never seen before. What is more, the effortless flow of thoughts, images and memories was not muddied by the usual conceits and vanities. What was most striking of all, however, is that he spoke about himself with a freedom and candour that suggested a degree of personal, inner liberation I hadn't suspected. It was a powerful contrast to the awkward, halting revelation on that Donkin bench forty years earlier.

The story I pieced together was not an uncommon one: a lonely and confused childhood, a powerful father who didn't understand, a mother who did but tried too hard to protect, and a society that judged harshly and unjustly. At one point he stopped himself in full flight and grew thoughtful for a moment as he carefully stubbed out the half-smoked cigarette he had treated himself to. Then, with a smile: 'But what the hell, it doesn't really matter you know.' I asked him what he meant. 'The whole silly circus man! The juggling acts, the balancing acts, the tightropes we are always trying to walk ... and falling off. Always falling off! There's a play for you if you want one ... The Circus of Life!' He

*'Garth always stands very straight
– even as a schoolboy he is "at attention" '*

paused again while he relit the cigarette stub, his face – half lit by his
bedside lamp – folding up in satisfaction, his eyes closed, as he took his
first drag and pulled the smoke down as deeply as he could into his
lungs. It was a moment of still and quiet life, and I somehow knew it
was a closing image of my cousin. I tried my best to record every detail
of it: the jacket of his second-hand brown suit draped over the back of
his chair, the crumpled soft collar of his white shirt, his loosened tie –
grey and maroon diagonal stripes, khaki braces, paunch and unsteady
hands, and behind him on the wall the Sacred Heart of Jesus.

I left him that night with the suggestion that he should try putting his
story down on paper. It wasn't that I had any high literary hopes for the

96

outcome of the exercise, but because he had complained bitterly once again of boredom and having nothing with which to occupy a still very active and alert mind. As it turned out our reunion was to have literary consequences on my side as well. I didn't realise it at the time but the seed for this memoir had been planted that night. Driving back in lashing rain along De Waal Drive to my Sea Point flat, I found myself gathering together all the images I had of his disturbing and provocative presence in my childhood. Later that night when I was entering them in my notebook and remembering other incidents in my childhood, it suddenly dawned on me how profound and still unacknowledged was the debt I owed to my two cousins. I couldn't believe or explain why it had taken me so long to realise it. When I resumed writing – memories of Johnnie now going into my notebook as well – it was to do so as feverishly as the young Hally of fifty years earlier dashing off a twenty-page English composition for Doc Bromley. That particular notebook entry ends with this:

> 'Must ask Garth about his memory of that night on the Donkin bench.'

I never got a chance to do so. Quite unexpectedly my last few days in Cape Town became very busy, and I left for Johannesburg without getting a chance to see him again.

It was some months later when I was back in America and in rehearsals for the New York production of *The Road to Mecca*, that the telegram arrived with the news of his death from a heart attack. I have always had a hugely delayed reaction to death, even when the person was very close to me. To date the three major losses in my life have been father and mother and then Yvonne Bryceland, and with all of them it took a lot of time before their passing became a hard and indisputable fact and I finally understood and accepted that all I had left were the memories. When that happened, instead of a flood of emotion, my reaction has been a kind of dry, aching disbelief together with a bitter anger with myself for all the opportunities for truth and love I had wasted when they were alive. In the case of Garth's death – and there is no way our relationship could be described as 'close' – my response was further blunted by the pressures of a New York opening. I eventually tried to deal with it and make it real about nine months later when I returned to South Africa and I found waiting for me in Port Elizabeth a plain cardboard box containing his last personal possessions. His Good Samaritan friend in Cape Town had forwarded it.

My first cursory examination of its contents revealed a jumble of Bibles and prayer books – a Salvation Army hymn book among them, a few personal papers, an album of photographs, and the start of the autobiography I had suggested to him. I opened one of the Bibles and a piece of paper fell out. On it was written – in his handwriting – the Catholic prayer: 'Lighten our darkness we beseech thee Oh Lord; and by Thy great mercy defend us from all perils and dangers of this night for the love of thy only son, our Saviour Jesus Christ.' The next item out of the box was the school medal awarded to his mother, Aunt Dulcie, for unbroken school attendance between the years 1900 and 1907. I couldn't go any further. The thought that those three lives, with all their passion and fury and love, had run dry of consequences and ended up as these pathetic oddments in a cardboard box left me feeling very depressed. I closed it up and packed it away. It is only now, about two years later, that I have sat down with it again and examined its contents carefully.

The photograph album belonged to his mother and in it I found my first images of Garth Nixon Fugard as a little boy, gangling teenager, innocent young recruit in the Royal Army Medical Corps in 1937 and then finally in khaki shorts, shirt and bush hat, as ageing scoutmaster surrounded by young boys also in scouting uniform.

It also produced the only family photograph of son, mother and father. These photographs have helped me to see clearly and define a quality in my cousin that I had only been vaguely aware of before. The word that comes to mind is 'pride'. (I've looked at enough photographs of myself to know that I don't have it. On the other hand, my brother does, and so did my father.) Knowing that he is being photographed Garth always stands very straight – even as a schoolboy he is 'at attention' – and he stares back steadily and seriously at the camera. There are no silly smiles here; the camera is recording the moment for

'There are no silly smiles here'

posterity and he knows it. In paging through the album another strong word suggested itself: 'brave'. I also know enough about cowardice to believe there wasn't a vestige of it in my cousin. The image of another man, a stranger comes to mind: He was in the dock of a Johannesburg courtroom and he was facing up to a harsh sentence – he had just been declared a habitual criminal – with the same unflinching, shoulders back and chin up courage I see in the photographs of my cousin. It is a perfect metaphor for Garth – in all my memories of him, from the wild young man with a tumbler of brandy in his hand and a Salvation Army uniform at the ready, through to the elderly bachelor in his little back room nursing a heart condition and dying of boredom, he knew he was standing in life's dock facing judgement and sentence, and he was very brave about it.

And then finally his autobiography: one hundred and twenty-six foolscap pages of small spidery writing. Title: *A Can of Worms*. The author Jack Lanigan (pseudonym for Garth Nixon Fugard). There is also a dedication: 'To my cousin Athol, who persuaded me to take the lid off this can of worms.' Here is the first page:

'I was born on October 22nd, 1918. The whole world was then being swept by a killer influenza virus to which countless graveyards can bear witness throughout the world. Whole populations were wiped out in some remote areas. As was to be my lifetime pattern, my mother did not have flu when I appeared, but pneumonia. You see I just had to be different. I always have been in more ways than one, as you shall see. The place was Port Elizabeth in the Eastern Province of what was then the Union of South Africa.

'My father had also been born there. Mother was from England. They had met during the First World War when she was a nurse in a large military hospital in France and Dad had been brought in with a piece of shrapnel in his head. It remained there all his life, being too near the brain for the surgeons of those days to risk removing it. As a youngster I never realised that it probably accounted for his violent rages, particularly after he had had a few drinks too many. He was a periodic alcoholic, often the worst kind for those who have to live with them.

'My earliest recollection, I could not have been more than about two and a half to three years old, is of my father, very drunk and in a flaming rage, trying to strangle my mother as they struggled and swayed about the bedroom. I stood up in a cot absolutely terrified. I think most psychologists will agree that the effect upon a small child could have implications which would have lasting effects. My uncle Harold, younger than my father, tried to intervene, which was very brave for a cripple. When sober he was a most loving and understanding father. A love-hate relationship was established between us until, to my lasting regret, he was a sick old man, blind and suffering from Parkinson's disease.

'When I was three-and-a-half years of age my parents separated. That separation was to last nine-and-a-half years.'

When I had suggested to Garth that he try to tell his story on paper I had also urged him to be open and completely frank about his homosexuality. Reading through his one hundred and twenty-six pages it was very moving to see with what courage, albeit a little coyly, he had responded to my challenge. Here is an incident at school during his childhood:

'A strange incident happened while I was there. I have often wondered what a psychologist with a foreknowledge of my life yet to come, would make of it. My little pal then was a boy named Colin, Colin Davis to be precise. One day we were in the cloakroom together, alone. I even remember that Colin was wearing a furry pullover; strange, I have all my life liked to see people wearing them. We hugged each other. 'Colin,' I whispered, 'when we grow up let's get married.' No comment. But as my story progresses perhaps you will remember this little cameo of childhood. I have often.'

And then later, aged nineteen and still a raw recruit in the RAMC:

'...disaster struck in a way of which I should never have dreamed in my most fantastic nightmares. I went to watch a football match between men from our camp and villagers from Chisledon Village. It was held in a field surrounded by high hedgerows and green hollows. I went to that soccer game as innocent a youngster as you could find anywhere and came away very, very deeply shocked and a totally changed personality. To put it bluntly – I was raped by a very tough member of a Highland regiment. At first I had absolutely no idea what he was after – when I did it was too late. Terrified of causing a scene by shouting for help, as embarrassed as it was possible to get, and very, very frightened indeed of this hard-case old soldier, I submitted.'

Just before the outbreak of the Second World War, Garth's RAMC unit was sent to Palestine. It was there that he met the one great soulmate of his life, young Michael Hall Smith who was in the Black Watch. Garth's memoir insists that the deep friendship that developed between them involved no homosexuality:

'We became quite a joke. My lot dubbed us the Siamese twins. What one wanted to do, so did the other. Where one went, what one thought, so did the other. My mates put an entirely wrong interpretation on this friendship of ours ...

'One of the things which bonded us together was the fact that we had both experienced unhappy early teens. Michael's stepfather was a London stockbroker who simply was not interested in his existence and had put him in the Second Black Watch Boys Service. When I met him he was just coming into what was called 'man's service', at the age of seventeen and a half. We were that peculiar example of two basic loners coming together. I am stressing all this because my almost abnormal affection for Michael was to play a tremendous part in my life for years to come. We were the David and Jonathan of the Bible. All too tragically, that comparison was to be carried to its bitter conclusion.'

Separation was inevitable. Michael ended up on Crete and Garth at the North African frontline. It was there that he received the news of Michael's death from a German sniper's bullet. In a case of 'delayed-reaction' the emotional breakdown only came months later, not long after the battle of El Alamein in October 1942.

'What was the worst thing I saw in the desert war? What was the one thing that reduced me to tears? Not charred bodies half-hanging out of burnt out tanks. Not a pit full of amputations. Not men shocked out of their minds by shelling. You become almost immune to these things.

'What then?

'A child's broken doll!!

'The war in the Egyptian and Libyan deserts was over. It had been a war of man against man, machine against machine, such as the world had never seen before. It was utterly divorced from what we could call normal civilian life, except for the usually forgotten people who had lived in the coastal towns through which the warring armies had swept like a whirlwind. Many of us had reached breaking point, myself among them.

'One day our unit came upon the most idyllic scene one could have imagined: a beautiful Italian settler's farm. Blossoming almond trees stood in rows amid luscious green grass. White sheep grazed and lambs gambolled. Peacocks strutted and displayed their gorgeous tail feathers. With another man, I went into the farmhouse. All around our feet lay debris. The home, for a home it was, had been hastily evacuated. I opened the door of an inner room. Lying on the floor was a small broken doll. Somewhere a child would be crying for it.

'With him things were never what they appeared to be'

'I burst into tears. All the pent up emotions of years came to the surface at once. For the first time since war had broken out I had realised that war involved nice decent home-loving folk as well as soldiers. For me it was the start of a nervous breakdown. No, not the start. The seeds had been sown long years ago… Michael's death had soaked deep into my soul and I had had no spiritual reserves to turn to. It was to be many many years before I found them and by then, as in that Italian farmer's house, a lifetime's debris would be left behind.'

From then on *A Can of Worms* becomes a catalogue of the time spent in the mental wards of various military hospitals until his eventual discharge from the army in Pretoria in June 1943. It stops coincidentally

The final snapshot of Garth
'A Fugard behind the pasty, sagging features'

and very frustratingly just before he and I are due to meet in the Jubilee Hotel for the first time. I don't believe there is any significance in that; I am sure it was his death that broke it off there. What is obvious now of course is that the wild and wayward presence that drifted in and out of my childhood was a man suffering from what we used to call shellshock, the Post Traumatic Stress Syndrome of modern psychology. I also understand now why I heard echoes of his unnerving laugh all through the writing of *Playland.* My portrait of Gideon le Roux owes a lot more than I had realised to my timely reunion with Garth just before his death.

I've already mentioned how depressed I was by my first encounter with that miserable cardboard box of 'personal possessions'. When I

The author and cousin Johnnie,
photographed in Johannesburg in 1994

reached the end of Garth's memoir, turned the last of those 126 hand-written pages in the old fashioned office file, I discovered that my feelings about it had changed. In telling his story he had invested that box and its contents with a simple and moving dignity; humble though it might be it was evidence now of a life that had been lived. As I packed away its contents I experienced a quiet sense of relief and release. The image of my cousin, bent over his stack of cheap paper in his little room, his heater out of its hiding place in the wardrobe, plugged in for a little surreptitious warmth as he scribbled his way through a Cape winter and his memories of the sixty-seven years that lay behind him, that picture of him was one with which I felt a powerful and joyous kinship. After all that is no more or less than what I have been doing for some months now with the writing of this memoir: trying, like him, to tell my story. In his *Messingkauf Dialogues* Brecht puts these words in the mouth of his philosopher: '... lamenting by means of sounds, or better still words, is a vast liberation, because it means that the sufferer is beginning to produce something. He's already mixing his sorrow with an account of the blows he had received; he's already making something out of the utterly devastating.' That is surely what Garth had done.

So then finally to complete the picture, let me also evoke an image of Johnnie. Even as I am writing he might be sitting at his piano in a little Eastern Transvaal town transforming all that life has meant to him into the sound of his music. Three cousins connected finally by something even deeper than our blood ties, the three of us all dabblers in that most mysterious of all the processes of the soul, the one and only true alchemy, the transformative, trying to turn the substance of our very ordinary lives into something enduring and special. If anything defines us for what we are, it is surely that: and whether it is with a foxtrot or the frescoes of the Sistine Chapel that we try to do it, that is our hopeless and splendid endeavour, our attempt to defeat the high, imprisoning walls of our mortality.